CHILDREN'S PARTY COOKING

Carole Handslip

CHANCELLOR
PRESS

CONTENTS

First published in Great Britain in 1983

This edition published in 1993 by Chancellor Press
an imprint of Reed Consumer Books Limited
Michelin House, 81 Fulham Road, London SW3 6RB
and Auckland, Melbourne, Singapore and Toronto

Reprinted 1993

Copyright © 1983 Reed International Books Limited

ISBN 1 85152 323 5

A CIP catalogue record for this book is available from the
British Library

Printed in China

INTRODUCTION

Children's parties – for whatever age – should be fun. Plan well in advance and you'll enjoy the preparation and the party. Everything must be bright, colourful and gay, so there's plenty of room for imaginative ideas. The party themes and foods suggested here may be interchanged to suit your children.

Decide on the party theme and what you want to serve, then make a list and spend a few hours shopping for the food and accessories you need, including paper plates, cups, napkins, straws and candles. This will eliminate any last-minute panic over forgotten items.

Much of the food can be cooked in advance. Don't overdo quantities – younger children are usually too excited to eat very much, while older ones will be busy dancing. Have plenty of crisps and savoury snacks around – all age groups like nibbling – but don't open too many at once or the food may not get eaten.

Place names are a great help for a sit-down tea. Your child will probably enjoy making these with coloured card and felt-tipped pens, following the party theme. For younger children, names piped on chocolate fingers or small biscuits make fun place settings.

Whatever age you're catering for the cake is the centrepiece of the table and worth every minute you spend on it: the children will really appreciate your efforts. Don't worry if your icing isn't perfect – they won't! Relax – and enjoy their pleasure and fun.

NOTES

Standard spoon measures are used in all recipes
1 tablespoon=one 15 ml spoon
1 teaspoon=one 5 ml spoon
All spoon measures are level unless otherwise stated.

Eggs used in the recipes are standard size, i.e. size 3, unless otherwise stated. If large eggs are specified, use size 1.

Fresh herbs are used unless otherwise stated. If unobtainable substitute a bouquet garni of the equivalent dried herbs, or use dried herbs instead but halve the quantities stated.

Use freshly ground black pepper where pepper is specified.

Recipes for basic sponge, pastries, apricot glaze, and butter, moulding and glacé icings (marked with an asterisk) are given on pages 92-3.

For all recipes, quantities are given in both metric and imperial measures. Follow either set but not a mixture of both, because they are not interchangeable.

TINY TOTS PARTY

Parties for younger children are lots of fun – but very hard work! Try to enlist the help of children between the ages of 12 and 16: they seem to have a gift for dealing with tiny children. Use coloured paper cups, plates and napkins to give the party atmosphere – and make the clearing up easier, too.

All the food should be made with an eye to colour and size. It's far better to make lots of tiny mouthfuls than have a table full of half-nibbled leftovers. Cocktail sausages, crisps and similar savoury snacks are all popular. Sandwiches especially should be very small and presented in an unusual way, such as the Sandwich House and Pinwheel Sandwiches. Use sweet or savoury fillings, depending on what your children like: banana, marmite, peanut butter and cheese are all popular. Make them in the morning, cover with clingfilm and refrigerate until required.

Keep the birthday cake fairly simple: the Engine is ideal – it's easy to make, covered with chocolate icing and very colourful. When making the cake, it's a good idea to add an extra 1-egg quantity and make 24 little Smartie Buns.

This menu, which serves six, is ideal for 3- to 5-year-olds. Most of the foods can be prepared in advance and stored in the freezer. The Cheese Twigs, Traffic Light Biscuits and White Mice can be stored in airtight tins for several days.

This age group is far more interested in the tea than anything else, so all the effort you put into it will be worthwhile. The table – and the guests – may look a mess at the end, but you'll know they've enjoyed it!

Cheese Twigs

125 g (4 oz) plain
  flour
pinch of salt
50 g (2 oz) butter or
  margarine
75 g (3 oz) Cheddar
  cheese, coarsely
  grated
1 Oxo cube, roughly
  crumbled
1 egg yolk
2-3 teaspoons water

Sift the flour and salt into a bowl. Rub in the fat until the mixture resembles breadcrumbs. Stir in the cheese and Oxo cube, then add the egg yolk and enough water to mix to a firm dough.

Turn onto a floured surface and knead lightly. Roll out thinly into a large square, about 5 mm (¼ inch) thick. Cut into strips 5 mm (¼ inch) wide and 7.5 cm (3 inches) long.

Place on baking sheets and bake in a preheated moderately hot oven, 200°C (400°F), Gas Mark 6, for 8 to 10 minutes, until golden.

Makes about 80

Sandwich House

10 large slices brown
  bread
20-30 cheese twigs
  (see above)
1 celery stick, cut into
  thin strips
1 teaspoon chopped
  parsley
parsley sprigs
1 carrot
1-2 teaspoons cream
  cheese
FILLING:
25 g (1 oz) soft
  margarine
50 g (2 oz) cream
  cheese
1 × 120 g (4¼ oz)
  can sardines in
  tomato sauce
salt and pepper

For the filling, beat the margarine with the cream cheese, sardines and their sauce, and salt and pepper to taste. Use to make up 5 rounds of sandwiches and remove the crusts.

Cut 2 rounds into 6 oblongs. Place the 2 cut rounds on top of each other on a cake board to make an oblong.

Cut the remaining sandwiches into 12 triangles. Place 8 triangles on top of the oblong to form a roof. Arrange the cheese twigs along either side.

Cut the remaining bread triangles in half and arrange in front as a fence. Lay the celery in the 'garden' and sprinkle with chopped parsley to represent grass. Position parsley sprigs for bushes.

Cut pieces of carrot for the door, windows and chimney. Use a small fluted cutter to make carrot flowers. Use a little cream cheese to stick on the door and windows; place a blob on the chimney to represent smoke.

Serves 8

NOTE: Use any fillings you like for this house: marmite, peanut butter and sandwich spreads are all popular.

Egg and Bacon Tartlets

125 g (4 oz)
  shortcrust pastry*
75 g (3 oz) streaky
  bacon, derinded
  and chopped
1 large egg
5 tablespoons milk
25 g (1 oz) Cheddar
  cheese, grated
salt and pepper
pinch of dry mustard

Roll out the dough thinly on a floured surface and use to line twelve 7.5 cm (3 inch) patty tins; chill for 15 minutes.

Place the bacon in a small pan and fry gently in its own fat until beginning to turn golden. Beat the egg and milk together in a bowl, beat in the cheese, then stir in the bacon. Season with salt, pepper and mustard to taste. Divide between the pastry cases.

Bake in a preheated moderately hot oven, 200°C (400°F), Gas Mark 6, for 15 to 20 minutes, until set and golden. **Makes 12**

Pinwheel Sandwiches

4 slices medium sliced
  brown bread, crusts
  removed
FILLING:
75 g (3 oz) cream
  cheese
1 tablespoon
  mayonnaise
salt and pepper
1 celery stick

For the filling, beat the cream cheese with the mayonnaise and salt and pepper to taste. Cut the celery into four 5 mm (¼ inch) sticks, the same length as the bread. Roll out the bread lightly with a rolling pin and spread thickly with the cheese filling. Place a stick of celery across one end of each slice. Roll up tightly, pressing the edge down firmly. Wrap in cling film and chill until required.

    Cut the rolls into 1 cm (½ inch) slices to serve.

Makes about 32

Lemonade

4 lemons
75 g (3 oz) caster
  sugar
1.2 litres (2 pints)
  boiling water

Finely grate the rind from the lemons and place in a heatproof jug with the sugar. Pour over the water and stir until the sugar has dissolved. Squeeze the juice from the lemons and strain into the jug. Allow to cool, then chill.

Makes 1.5 litres (2½ pints)

Illustrated on page 3

Smartie Buns

50 g (2 oz) soft
   margarine
50 g (2 oz) caster
   sugar
50 g (2 oz) self-
   raising flour, sifted
pinch of baking
   powder
1 egg
TOPPING:
50 g (2 oz) glacé
   icing*
selection of food
   colourings
24 smarties

Place the cake ingredients in a mixing bowl and beat vigorously for 2 minutes, until thoroughly blended.

Arrange 24 petits fours cases on a baking sheet and two-thirds fill with mixture. Bake in a preheated moderate oven, 180°C (350°F), Gas Mark 4, for 15 minutes. Cool on a wire rack.

Divide the icing into several portions and colour each one with a few drops of colouring. Spoon a little icing onto the centre of each cake and top with a smartie.
Makes 24

Chocolate Milk

125 g (4 oz) plain
   chocolate, chopped
150 ml (¼ pint)
   boiling water
900 ml (1½ pints)
   milk

Place the chocolate and water in an electric blender or food processor and blend on maximum speed for 10 seconds. Add the milk and blend for a further 10 seconds. Allow to cool, then chill. Serve with straws.
Makes about 1.2 litres (2 pints)

Marshmallow Tarts

125 g (4 oz)
   shortcrust pastry*
2 tablespoons
   raspberry jam
2 tablespoons apricot
   jam
12 pink and white
   marshmallows
3 glacé cherries,
   quartered

Roll out the pastry thinly on a floured surface and use to line twelve 7.5 cm (3 inch) patty tins. Chill for 15 minutes.

Place a teaspoon of jam in each pastry case. Bake in a preheated moderately hot oven, 200°C (400°F), Gas Mark 6, for 10 to 15 minutes, until the pastry is golden.

Place a pink marshmallow on the raspberry tarts and a white one on the apricot tarts. Return to the oven for 1 minute to melt the marshmallow slightly. Transfer to a wire rack to cool. Place a piece of cherry in the centre of each tart.
Makes 12

Traffic Light Biscuits

25 g (1 oz) caster
   sugar
50 g (2 oz) butter or
   margarine
75 g (3 oz) plain
   flour, sifted
TOPPING:
50 g (2 oz) glacé
   icing*
few drops each of red,
   yellow and green
   food colouring
1 tablespoon red jam

Beat the sugar and fat together until light and fluffy. Add the flour and mix until the mixture binds together.

Turn onto a floured surface and knead until smooth. Roll out to an oblong 4 mm (3/16 inch) thick and cut into 2.5 × 7.5 cm (1 × 3 inch) strips. Cut out 3 circles with a 1.5 cm (3/4 inch) pastry cutter or piping nozzle from each of half the strips.

Place all the strips on baking sheets and bake in a preheated moderate oven, 160°C (325°F), Gas Mark 3, for 15 to 20 minutes, until pale golden. Leave to cool on the baking sheets.

Divide the icing into 3 portions and colour each with a food colouring. Spread the plain biscuits with a thin layer of jam. Place the biscuits with holes in on top. Fill the holes with the coloured icing to represent the traffic lights.
Makes about 9

Fruit Jelly Rabbit

1 raspberry jelly
1 banana
50 g (2 oz) grapes,
   halved and pipped
50 g (2 oz)
   raspberries

Make up the jelly with 450 ml (¾ pint) boiling water (or as directed on the packet) and allow to cool.

Slice the banana and add to the jelly with the grapes and raspberries. Turn into a 750 ml (1¼ pint) rabbit mould and leave to set. Dip quickly into hot water to unmould.

Serves 6 to 8

NOTE: To serve more children, make up a lime jelly. Allow to set, then chop finely. Arrange around the rabbit to represent grass.

White Mice

2 egg whites
125 g (4 oz) caster
   sugar
24 split almonds
36 coloured 'silver'
   balls
few red liquorice
   bootlaces, cut into
   10 cm (4 inch)
   lengths

Whisk the egg whites until stiff and dry looking. Whisk in the sugar, a tablespoon at a time, and continue whisking until very thick.

Spoon into a piping bag fitted with a 1 cm (½ inch) plain nozzle. Line a baking sheet with non-stick paper and pipe the mixture into mounds, wide at one end and tapering off to a point at the other; neaten with a palette knife if necessary. Place the almonds in the tapered end for ears. Position the balls for eyes and nose.

Bake in a preheated very cool oven, 110°C (225°F), Gas Mark ¼, for 2 hours. Cool on the baking sheets.

Make a small hole in the tail end of each mouse with a skewer and stick in a piece of liquorice to make a tail.

Makes 12

Chocolate Rocks

2 tablespoons clear
   honey
25 g (1 oz) margarine
125 g (4 oz) plain
   chocolate
125 g (4 oz) bran
   flakes

Place the honey, margarine and chocolate in a pan and stir over a low heat until melted. Add the bran flakes and mix thoroughly until well coated. Spoon into paper cases and leave to set.

Makes about 15

CHRISTMAS PARTY

In many ways a Christmas party is easier to cope with. The house will already be looking festive with the Christmas tree, decorations and cards, while much of the party food can be prepared along with other Christmas fare.

There are lots of exciting plates, cups, napkins and table decorations available at this time. Crackers give a festive touch and place names made out of green card and cut into the shape of Christmas trees are fun.

The suggested menu is suitable for twelve 4- to 8-year-old children, but Christmas is an excuse for a party for any child – just choose foods to suit the age

group. For young children, the same general guidelines apply as for the Tiny Tots party.

The Ice Cream Clowns are very effective and popular but do make them well in advance so they can harden. All you have to do to serve is stand them on the biscuits and pop their hats on.

The cake for this party could be the Christmas Tree or, for a smaller number, the Post Box. The Christmas Tree is very easy to ice and decorate; the left-over pieces can be used to make truffles or trifle.

If you choose the Post Box, pipe the child's name on the front panel to make it personal. You will need to turn the cake on its side for piping and cutting. The addition of a robin and snow makes it festive.

Celery Boats

113 g (4 oz) cream
   cheese
1 tablespoon chopped
   chives
salt and pepper
1 head of celery,
   divided into sticks
TO FINISH:
rice paper
cocktail sticks
few lettuce leaves,
   shredded

Place the cheese in a bowl with the chives and salt and pepper to taste. Mix well until smooth. Spoon a little of the mixture into each celery stick and spread smoothly. Cut into 6 cm (2½ inch) lengths.

Cut the rice paper into triangles, spear with a cocktail stick and stick into the celery.

Arrange the lettuce on a serving dish and place the celery boats on top.
Makes about 20

Tuna Tugs

1 × 198 g (7 oz) can
   tuna fish, drained
50 g (2 oz) soft
   margarine
3 tablespoons
   mayonnaise
salt and pepper
12 small bridge rolls,
   halved
¼ cucumber
1 carrot
24 strips cucumber
   peel (optional)

Place the tuna fish in a bowl and mash with a fork. Add the margarine, mayonnaise, and salt and pepper to taste. Mix with a fork until smooth. Place 2 teaspoons of the mixture on each half roll and smooth to the edges.

Cut the cucumber into 1 cm (½ inch) sticks and place vertically on each roll. Cut the carrot into 2.5 cm (1 inch) sticks and place in front of the cucumber as funnels. Wrap the cucumber peel around the tugs, if using.
Makes 24

Marmite Bites

215 g (7½ oz)
   packet frozen puff
   pastry, thawed
1 tablespoon marmite
½ teaspoon water

Roll out the pastry thinly on a floured surface to a rectangle about 25 × 30 cm (10 × 12 inches). Mix the marmite and water together and spread over the pastry to cover completely.
Roll up loosely from the shorter side like a Swiss roll; position the join underneath. Chill for 20 minutes.

Cut into 5 mm (¼ inch) slices, place on baking sheets and make a slit in each from edge to centre. Bake in a preheated moderately hot oven, 200°C (400°F), Gas Mark 6, for 10 minutes or until golden. Serve warm or cold.
Makes about 30

Chessboard Sandwiches

8 slices brown bread
8 slices white bread
FILLINGS:
50 g (2 oz) butter
6 tablespoons
  mayonnaise
3 hard-boiled eggs,
  finely chopped
50 g (2 oz) cream
  cheese
75 g (3 oz) Cheddar
  cheese, grated
2 tablespoons
  chopped chives
salt and pepper

For the fillings, beat the butter with the mayonnaise; divide in half. Stir the chopped eggs into one portion; mix the cheeses and chives into the other portion. Season both with salt and pepper to taste.

Make the sandwiches using one slice of brown bread, one slice of white and one filling for each. Remove the crusts, then cut each sandwich into 4 squares.

Arrange them in two layers on a square cake board, alternating the brown and white side to create a chessboard effect.
Makes 32

Cola Float

1.75 litres (3 pints)
  cola
12 scoops vanilla
  easy scoop ice cream

Three-quarters fill 12 beakers with cola, then place a scoop of ice cream on top. Serve with straws.
Serves 12

Porcupines

2 oranges or
   grapefruit
150 g (5 oz) Cheddar
   cheese, cubed
1 × 227 g (8 oz) can
   pineapple pieces,
   drained
50 cocktail sticks
2 stuffed olives,
   halved crosswise
1 small gherkin,
   halved
20 cocktail sausages,
   grilled

Cut a slice off one side of each fruit so they will stand firmly.

Thread cheese and pineapple onto cocktail sticks, and stick into one fruit to make the porcupine's spikes.

Pierce 2 olive halves and 1 gherkin piece with halved cocktail sticks. Push them into the fruit to make the porcupine's eyes and nose.

Place a sausage on each of the remaining cocktail sticks and stick them into the other fruit. Make the eyes and nose in the same way.
Makes 2 'porcupines'

Orange and Pineapple Drink

4 oranges
50 g (2 oz) caster
   sugar
1.2 litres (2 pints)
   boiling water
600 ml (1 pint)
   pineapple juice
orange slices to decorate

Finely grate the rind from the oranges and place in a heatproof jug. Add the sugar and water and stir until the sugar has dissolved. Squeeze the juice from the oranges and strain into the jug. Cool, then add the pineapple juice; chill. Serve topped with orange slices.
Makes 2 litres (3½ pints)

Ice Cream Clowns

2 litres (3½ pints)
   vanilla easy scoop
   ice cream
60 smarties
12 liquorice comfits
12 jelly beans
2 tablespoons
   chocolate sugar
   strands
2 tablespoons leftover
   butter icing*
12 ice cream cones
12 chocolate biscuits

Chill a baking sheet in the freezer for 10 minutes. Using a large ice cream scoop, make 12 ice cream balls. Arrange them on the baking sheet and return to the freezer for 1 hour.

Working quickly, press on smarties for eyes and comfits for nose and mouth. Return to freezer for 3 hours.

Spread icing around the top of each ice cream cone and dip in chocolate strands. Put 3 dots of icing on each cone and stick a smartie on each one. Arrange the biscuits on a serving dish and place an ice cream ball on each. Top with an ice cream cone 'clown's hat' and serve immediately.
Makes 12

Meringue Mushrooms

2 egg whites
125 g (4 oz) caster
   sugar
1 lime jelly
3 tablespoons double
   cream, whipped
25 g (1 oz) plain
   chocolate, grated

Whisk the egg whites until stiff, then whisk in 2 tablespoons of the sugar. Carefully fold in the remaining sugar.

Spoon the mixture into a piping bag fitted with a 1 cm (½ inch) plain nozzle. Line a baking sheet with non-stick paper and pipe 5 cm (2 inch) meringue mounds for the mushroom heads, and 2 cm (¾ inch) mounds for stalks. Bake in a preheated very cool oven, 110°C (225°F), Gas Mark ¼, for about 2 hours, until crisp and dry. Allow to cool.

Meanwhile, make up the jelly with 450 ml (¾ pint) boiling water, as directed on the packet. When set firmly, turn onto a sheet of grease-proof paper and chop finely. Spread on a large plate to represent grass.

Scoop out a hollow with a sharp knife on the underside of the larger meringues. Place a little cream in each hollow and attach the 'stalks'. Sprinkle over the chocolate and arrange the mushrooms on the 'grass'.
Makes 10 to 12

Cherry Mince Pies

125 g (4 oz)
  shortcrust pastry*
FILLING:
175 g (6 oz)
  mincemeat
50 g (2 oz)
  maraschino
  cherries, drained
  and quartered
1 teaspoon lemon juice
MERINGUE:
1 egg white
50 g (2 oz) caster
  sugar
TO DECORATE:
3 maraschino cherries,
  quartered

Roll out the pastry thinly on a floured surface and use to line twelve 7.5 cm (3 inch) patty tins. Prick the bases well and chill for 15 minutes.

Press a piece of foil into each pastry case and bake blind in a preheated moderately hot oven, 200°C (400°F), Gas Mark 6, for 10 to 15 minutes. Remove the foil and return to the oven for 2 minutes.

Mix together the filling ingredients. Divide between the pastry cases.

Whisk the egg white until stiff, then whisk in the sugar a tablespoon at a time. Spoon into a piping bag fitted with a 1 cm (½ inch) fluted nozzle and pipe a rosette on top of each pie. Top with the cherry pieces.

Bake in a preheated moderate oven, 180°C (350°F), Gas Mark 4, for 6 minutes or until golden. Serve warm or cold.
Makes 12

Gingerbread People

125 g (4 oz) plain
  flour
½ teaspoon
  bicarbonate of soda
½ teaspoon ground
  ginger
½ teaspoon ground
  cinnamon
25 g (1 oz) butter or
  margarine
50 g (2 oz) soft brown
  sugar
2 tablespoons golden
  syrup
1 teaspoon milk
50 g (2 oz) stiff glacé
  icing*

Sift the flour, soda and spices into a bowl. Place the fat, sugar and syrup in a pan over low heat until melted. Cool, then mix into the flour with the milk to make a firm dough. Wrap in polythene and chill for 30 minutes.

Turn the dough onto a floured surface and roll out to a 5 mm (¼ inch) thickness. Using gingerbread cutters, cut out 12 figures and place on greased baking sheets.

Bake in a preheated moderate oven, 160°C (325°F), Gas Mark 3, for 10 to 15 minutes, until firm. Transfer to a wire rack to cool.

Spoon the icing into a greaseproof paper piping bag fitted with a writing nozzle and pipe eyes, nose, mouth, buttons and borders on each figure.
Makes 12

Chocolate Nuggets

50 g (2 oz)
  margarine
175 g (6 oz) plain
  chocolate
2 tablespoons clear
  honey
250 g (8 oz)
  digestive biscuits,
  crushed
16 smarties

Place the margarine, chocolate and honey in a saucepan and heat gently until melted. Stir in the biscuit crumbs and mix thoroughly.

Turn into a greased and lined shallow 18 cm (7 inch) square cake tin and smooth the top. Mark into squares with a sharp knife and place a smartie in the centre of each. Leave to set, then cut into squares.

Makes 16

FANCY DRESS PARTY

Children love dressing up but it can be a bit of a chore for the parents – who have to find the costumes! It's a good idea therefore to give the party a theme, then those children and parents who have plenty of imagination can go to town, while even the least adventurous child will probably be able to think of a simple outfit with this guideline.

Whatever theme you choose, make the table as bright and colourful as possible. The chosen theme here is a Pirates' Party for twelve 6- to 10-year-olds. For this, you can have 'skull and crossbones' place names and serve the food from treasure chests and paper boats. A box overflowing with gold-wrapped chocolate coins would make a suitable finale.

The food suggested for this party can be used at other fancy dress parties and given appropriate names. For example, Pirate Sandwiches can become Phantom Fodder at a ghost's tea; Cannon Balls can become Desert Delights for an Arabian party.

As children get older, appetites increase so the food can be made a little larger and more unusual.

Piquant savoury flavours will be very popular, but children still like to know what they're eating. Open sandwiches are especially good for this reason, as are Pizza Scones. Small ordinary scones are successful, too: halve them and spread with different toppings, such as banana, egg, cheese or fish. Iced biscuits are always admired. They can be decorated in so many different ways the variety and choice is endless.

The novelty cake for this party is the Pirate Galleon, a most effective cake which can be made in a variety of colours and finished with a piped border.

Pirate Sandwiches

1 French stick
125 g (4 oz) butter
TOPPINGS:
cottage cheese
ham
salami
liver sausage
sardines

GARNISHES:
hard-boiled egg slices
tomato slices
parsley sprigs
radish slices
olive slices
cucumber twists

Cut the French stick diagonally into 1 cm (½ inch) slices and spread with butter. Cut the chosen toppings to fit the slices of bread or spread to the edges. Choose appropriate garnishes to decorate.
Makes 20

Treasure Islands

250 g (8 oz) plain
    flour
1 teaspoon cream of
    tartar
½ teaspoon
    bicarbonate of soda
½ teaspoon salt
50 g (2 oz)
    margarine
120 ml (4 fl oz) milk
milk to glaze
TOPPING:
2 tablespoons oil
1 onion, chopped
½ teaspoon dried
    marjoram
1 × 397 g (14 oz)
    can tomatoes,
    drained and
    chopped
salt and pepper
150 g (5 oz)
    Cheddar cheese,
    grated

Sift the flour, cream of tartar, bicarbonate of soda and salt into a mixing bowl and rub in the margarine until the mixture resembles breadcrumbs. Add the milk and mix to a soft dough.

Turn onto a floured surface, knead lightly and roll out to a 1 cm (½ inch) thickness. Cut into 6 cm (2½ inch) rounds with a plain cutter. Place on a floured baking sheet and brush with milk. Bake in a preheated hot oven, 220°C (425°F), Gas Mark 7, for 10 to 12 minutes, until golden. Cool on a wire rack.

To make the topping, heat the oil in a pan, add the onion and fry until softened. Add the marjoram, tomatoes, and salt and pepper to taste and cook for 3 minutes.

Cut the scones in half and place a spoonful of the tomato mixture on each half. Sprinkle with the cheese and bake in a preheated moderately hot oven, 190°C (375°F), Gas Mark 5, for 12 to 15 minutes, until golden and bubbling. Serve immediately.
Makes 12 to 14

Pirate Puffs

CHOUX PASTRY:
50 g (2 oz) butter or margarine
150 ml (¼ pint) water
65 g (2½ oz) plain flour, sifted
2 eggs
50 g (2 oz) Cheddar cheese, grated
½ teaspoon dry mustard

FILLING:
25 g (1 oz) butter or margarine
25 g (1 oz) plain flour
175 ml (6 fl oz) milk
¼ teaspoon dry mustard
75 g (3 oz) Cheddar cheese, grated
2 tablespoons mayonnaise
1 tablespoon chopped parsley
salt and pepper

Melt the fat in a saucepan, add the water and bring to the boil. Add the flour all at once and beat until the mixture leaves the side of the pan. Cool slightly, then add the eggs one at a time, beating vigorously until smooth. Beat in the cheese and mustard. Place teaspoonfuls of the mixture well apart on dampened baking sheets.

Bake in a preheated hot oven, 220°C (425°F), Gas Mark 7, for 10 minutes, then lower the heat to 190°C (375°F), Gas Mark 5, and bake for a further 20 to 25 minutes, until crisp. Make a slit in the side of each puff and cool on a wire rack.

To make the filling, melt the fat in a small pan. Stir in the flour, then gradually stir in the milk. Bring to the boil, stirring, until thickened. Stir in the mustard, cheese, mayonnaise, parsley, and salt and pepper to taste. Allow to cool.

Spoon the cheese mixture into the puffs to serve.
Makes about 30

Caribbean Dip

227 g (8 oz) cream cheese
4 tablespoons natural yogurt
75 g (3 oz) ham, finely diced
6 tablespoons crushed pineapple, drained
salt and pepper

TO SERVE:
cauliflower
carrot
red pepper
green pepper
celery sticks

Place the cream cheese in a bowl and stir to soften, then gradually mix in the yogurt. Add the ham, pineapple, and salt and pepper to taste, and mix well.

Choose a selection of vegetables as liked from those listed. Cut the cauliflower into florets, and the other vegetables into sticks measuring about 1 × 7.5 cm (½ × 3 inches). Arrange in baskets.

Place the dip in 2 small bowls and serve with the vegetables.
Makes 450 ml (¾ pint)

Jelly Boats

4 large oranges
1 packet orange jelly,
   cut into squares
1 sheet rice paper
16 cocktail sticks

Cut the oranges in half crossways, then squeeze to extract the juice; strain into a jug. Using a small spoon, scrape out all the membrane and pith, being careful not to pierce the skin. Arrange the shells close together in an upright position on a baking sheet.

Place the jelly in a measuring jug and pour on 150 ml (¼ pint) boiling water; stir until dissolved. Add the orange juice and make up to 450 ml (¾ pint) with water if necessary. Cool slightly. Pour into the shells and chill until set. When firm cut in half with a sharp knife.

Cut the rice paper into triangles and spear with a cocktail stick, then arrange one on each 'boat' as a sail.
Makes 16

Cannon Balls

250 g (8 oz) cake
   crumbs
125 g (4 oz)
   digestive biscuits,
   crushed
2 tablespoons cocoa
   powder
6 tablespoons clear
   honey
½ teaspoon rum
   essence
50 g (2 oz) chocolate
   sugar strands

Place the cake, biscuit crumbs and cocoa in a bowl and mix well. Add the honey and essence and mix to a stiff paste. Form into balls the size of a walnut.

Place the sugar strands in a small plastic bag and drop in the balls 3 at a time. Shake well until coated. Serve in petits fours paper cases, or other suitable containers.
Makes about 20

Buccaneer's Fizz

1 litre (1¾ pints)
   fruit cocktail drink
1.2 litres (2 pints)
   lemonade

Place the fruit juice in a jug and top up with lemonade. Serve with straws.
Makes 2 litres (3½ pints)

Pirates' Delight

900 ml (1½ pints)
  milk
1-2 tablespoons caster
  sugar
3 bananas, sliced

Place half the milk, sugar and bananas
in an electric blender or food
processor and blend on maximum
speed for 15 seconds. Repeat with
remaining ingredients. Serve with
straws.
Makes 1.25 litres (2¼ pints)

33

Golden Nuggets

50 g (2 oz) plain
  flour
pinch of salt
¼ teaspoon cayenne
  pepper
¼ teaspoon dry
  mustard
25 g (1 oz) butter or
  margarine
25 g (1 oz) Cheddar
  cheese, grated
1-2 tablespoons iced
  water
TOPPING:
40 g (1½ oz) butter
  or margarine
25 g (1 oz) rolled
  oats
40 g (1½ oz)
  Cheddar cheese,
  grated
¼ teaspoon mustard
  powder

Sift the flour, salt, cayenne and
mustard into a bowl and rub in the fat
until the mixture resembles
breadcrumbs. Stir in the cheese and
add enough water to mix to a firm
dough. Turn onto a floured surface
and knead lightly until smooth. Roll
out thinly and cut into 3.5 cm
(1½ inch) rounds with a plain cutter.
Place on a baking sheet and chill
while making the topping.

Cream the butter or margarine in a
bowl, add the remaining ingredients
and mix together thoroughly. Roll
the mixture into balls the size of a
cherry and press onto the pastry
rounds.

Bake in a preheated moderately hot
oven, 200°C (400°F), Gas Mark 6, for
12 to 15 minutes, until golden brown.
Cool on a baking sheet. Serve cold.
Makes 24

Jewel Biscuits

50 g (2 oz) plain
  flour
25 g (1 oz) butter or
  margarine
25 g (1 oz) caster
  sugar
beaten egg to mix
ICING:
50 g (2 oz) icing
  sugar, sifted
1-2 teaspoons warm
  water
selection of food
  colourings
TO DECORATE:
chocolate sugar strands
hundreds and
  thousands
jelly sweets
silver balls
sugar flowers

Sift the flour into a bowl and rub in
the fat until the mixture resembles
breadcrumbs. Stir in the sugar and
enough beaten egg to mix to a firm
dough.

Turn onto a floured surface and
knead until smooth. Roll out thinly
and cut into shapes using a small
fluted cutter, or diamond, star, heart
or animal-shaped cutters.

Place on a baking sheet and bake in
a preheated moderate oven, 180°C
(350°F), Gas Mark 4, for 12 to
15 minutes, until golden. Cool on the
baking sheet.

Place the icing sugar in a mixing
bowl and gradually add the water
until the icing coats the back of a
spoon thickly. Divide the icing into
portions and colour each as desired.

Spoon a little icing onto each
biscuit, spread almost to the edges
and decorate as desired.

Makes about 15

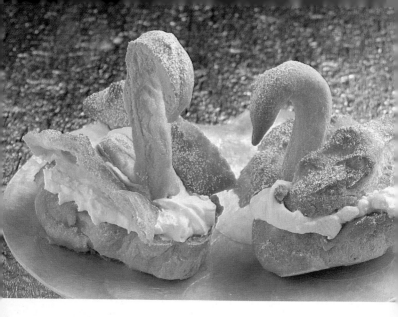

Silver Swans

CHOUX PASTRY:
75 g (3 oz) butter or
    margarine
200 ml (⅓ pint)
    water
125 g (4 oz) plain
    flour, sifted
3 large eggs, beaten
TO FINISH:
250 ml (8 fl oz)
    double cream
2 tablespoons icing
    sugar, sifted

Make the choux pastry (see page 92) and spoon into a piping bag fitted with an 8 mm (⅜ inch) plain nozzle.

Pipe 12 figure '2's for the necks, about 7.5 cm (3 inches) high, on a dampened baking sheet. Begin at the bottom and pull sharply away at the top to form the beak. Spoon the remaining pastry into rough oval shapes for the bodies, 7.5 cm (3 inches) long, on a second dampened baking sheet.

Bake in a preheated hot oven, 220°C (425°F), Gas Mark 7, for 10 minutes. Lower the heat to 190°C (375°F), Gas Mark 5, and bake for a further 10 minutes for the necks and 20 minutes for the bodies. Make a slit in the side of each; cool on a wire rack.

Using a sharp knife, cut each body in half horizontally. Cut the top half in half lengthways to form wings.

Whip the cream with half the icing sugar and spoon into the bottom halves of the bodies. Press a neck into the cream at one end and the wings into the cream on either side. Sprinkle with the remaining icing sugar.
Makes 12

Stowaway Bunnies

125 g (4 oz) caster
  sugar
2 tablespoons cocoa
  powder
2 egg whites
1 quantity Mint Ice
  Cream (see page
  46)
12 round chocolate
  mints, halved
36 chocolate drops

Mark twelve 7.5 cm (3 inch) circles
on non-stick paper and place on
2 baking sheets.

Sift the sugar and cocoa powder
together. Whisk the egg whites until
stiff and dry looking, then whisk in
half the sugar mixture 2 tablespoons
at a time. Fold in the rest.

Spoon the chocolate meringue onto
the circles and spread to the edges
with a palette knife. Bake in a
preheated very cool oven, 110°C
(225°F), Gas Mark ¼, for 2 hours.
Cool on the baking sheets.

Put the ice cream in the refrigerator
20 minutes before required to soften
slightly. Place a scoop of ice cream
on each meringue base. Place chocolate
mint halves on top to represent ears
and use chocolate drops for eyes and a
nose. Serve immediately.
Makes 12

BONFIRE PARTY

All children love a bonfire and the obvious excuse for a bonfire party is Hallowe'en or Guy Fawkes night. But any child about 8 to 12 years old with an autumn birthday will surely welcome such a novel birthday party.

This menu will serve 14 children and has been carefully chosen so that the food is easy to eat while standing round the fire. Serve hot Hallowe'en soup in mugs – it's easier to drink this way and is good for warming cold hands. Toffee apples are traditional at this time and just the thing to bite into whilst watching the flames leap into the sky. Popcornets are fun then too.

Gooey Chocolate Fudge Cakes and Chocolate Caramel Squares can be made in advance and stored in the freezer. These and the Mint Ice Cream Cornets could be served indoors later if preferred, when all the fun of the fire has finished and the children want to relax in the warm. A nice hot punch will be welcomed, too, either as a warm-up round the fire or when guests come indoors.

The Hallowe'en Cake is designed for this party and will provide the perfect finale to a fun-filled evening.

Hamburgers

1.5 kg (3½ lb)
  ground beef
2 large onions, finely
  chopped
4 tablespoons
  chopped parsley
1 tablespoon salt
2 tablespoons Worcester-
  shire sauce
pepper
14 hamburger buns
3 dill cucumbers,
  sliced lengthways
1 onion, thinly sliced

Mix the beef, onions, parsley, salt, sauce, and pepper to taste in a large bowl until thoroughly combined. Divide into 14 portions and shape each into a flat round about 2 cm (¾ inch) thick. Cook under a preheated hot grill for 3 minutes on each side.

Slice the buns in half and place a hamburger on the bottom half of each. Top with a few slices of dill cucumber and onion and cover with the top half of the bun. Serve with Corn Relish.
Makes 14

Corn Relish

4 tomatoes, skinned
  and chopped
1 onion, chopped
1 celery stick, chopped
4 tablespoons brown
  sugar
4 tablespoons malt
  vinegar
½ teaspoon mustard
  powder
salt and pepper
2 teaspoons cornflour
1 × 198 g (7 oz) can
  sweetcorn, drained

Place the tomatoes, onion, celery, sugar, vinegar, mustard, and salt and pepper to taste, in an enamel pan and simmer for 15 minutes.

Blend the cornflour with 2 tablespoons water and stir into the sauce with the sweetcorn. Bring to the boil, stirring occasionally, and boil until thickened. Leave to cool, then serve with Hamburgers, Crispy Sausages and Frankfurter and Bacon Rolls.
Makes 600 ml (1 pint)

Frankfurter and Bacon Rolls

14 frankfurters
4 processed cheese
  slices
14 rashers streaky
  bacon, derinded
14 bridge rolls, split
  open

Make a cut along each frankfurter, two thirds of the way through. Cut each slice of cheese into 4 strips and place one in each frankfurter.

Stretch the bacon with a palette knife and wind one rasher around each frankfurter to cover the cheese.

Cook under a preheated hot grill for 5 minutes, turning occasionally.

Place a frankfurter inside each roll. Serve with Corn Relish.
Serves 14

Hallowe'en Soup

2 tablespoons oil
2 onions, chopped
2 carrots, chopped
2 celery sticks,
    chopped
250 g (8 oz) swede,
    chopped
2 × 397 g (14 oz)
    cans tomatoes
1 tablespoon tomato
    purée
2 teaspoons salt
1 teaspoon soft brown
    sugar
1.5 litres (2½ pints)
    water
1 bouquet garni
pepper

Heat the oil in a large pan, add the onions and fry until softened. Stir in the carrots, celery, swede and the tomatoes with their juice.

Add the remaining ingredients, seasoning with pepper to taste. Bring to the boil, cover and simmer for 40 minutes, until the vegetables are tender. Cool slightly, remove the bouquet garni, then work in an electric blender or food processor until smooth. Serve hot, in mugs.

Makes 2.25 litres (4 pints)

Crispy Sausages

450 g (1 lb) chipolata
    sausages
4 tablespoons peanut
    butter
1 tablespoon French
    mustard
2-3 tablespoons water
16 thin slices brown
    bread, crusts
    removed
50 g (2 oz) soft
    margarine

Grill the sausages under a preheated hot grill, turning frequently, until browned all over. Put the peanut butter and mustard in a bowl, add the water and mix thoroughly. Roll the bread lightly with a rolling pin, then spread with the peanut mixture.

Place a sausage diagonally across each slice of bread and roll up tightly, securing with a cocktail stick. Spread each roll with margarine and place on a baking sheet. Bake in a preheated moderately hot oven, 200°C (400°F), Gas Mark 6, for 15 to 20 minutes, until golden. Serve with Corn Relish (see page 40).

Makes 16

NOTE: Butter may be used instead of peanut butter, in which case omit the water.

Hot Blackcurrant Punch

300 ml (½ pint)
  blackcurrant health
  drink
300 ml (½ pint)
  orange juice
1 teaspoon ground
  cinnamon
2.25 litres (4 pints)
  boiling water
1 orange, thinly sliced

Place the blackcurrant and orange
juices in a large heatproof jug. Blend
the cinnamon with a little of the
boiling water, then add to the jug
with the remaining water. Float the
orange slices on top. Serve in mugs.
Makes 2.75 litres (5 pints)

Bonfire Fizz

1.2 litres (2 pints)
  ginger beer
250 ml (8 fl oz)
  lemon squash
600 ml (1 pint) soda
  water
1 lemon, thinly sliced

Place the ginger beer and lemon squash in a large jug. Top up with the soda water and float the lemon slices on top.
Makes 2 litres (3½ pints)

Chocolate Fudge Cakes

125 g (4 oz) plain
  chocolate
300 ml (½ pint)
  milk
125 g (4 oz) soft
  brown sugar
125 g (4 oz) butter or
  margarine
125 g (4 oz) caster
  sugar
2 eggs, separated
250 g (8 oz) plain
  flour
1 teaspoon
  bicarbonate of soda
CHOCOLATE FUDGE
  ICING:
25 g (1 oz) butter or
  margarine
1-2 tablespoons milk
125 g (4 oz) icing
  sugar
1 tablespoon cocoa
  powder

Line and grease an 18 × 28 cm (7 × 11 inch) baking tin, allowing the paper to come 2.5 cm (1 inch) above 2 opposite sides.

Place the chocolate, 4 tablespoons of the milk and the brown sugar in a pan and heat gently, stirring, until melted. Stir in the remaining milk.

Cream the fat and caster sugar until light and fluffy, then beat in the egg yolks thoroughly.

Sift the flour and bicarbonate of soda together. Add to the creamed mixture with the chocolate mixture and beat until smooth. Whisk the egg whites until soft peaks form. Fold 1 tablespoon into the mixture to lighten it, then carefully fold in the rest.

Turn into the prepared tin and bake in a preheated moderate oven, 180°C (350°F), Gas Mark 4, for 50 minutes, until the cake springs back when lightly pressed. Turn onto a wire rack to cool slightly.

To make the icing, place the fat and 1 tablespoon milk in a small pan and heat gently until melted. Sift the icing sugar and cocoa together and add to the pan, mixing well until smooth; add a little more milk if necessary.

Pour over the warm cake and spread evenly to the edges. Allow to set completely, then cut into squares.
Makes 15

Chocolate Caramel Squares

125 g (4 oz) butter or
  margarine
50 g (2 oz) caster
  sugar
125 g (4 oz) plain
  flour
50 g (2 oz) ground
  rice
CARAMEL FILLING:
125 g (4 oz) butter or
  margarine
50 g (2 oz) caster
  sugar
2 tablespoons golden
  syrup
1 × 196 g (6.1 oz)
  can condensed milk
TOPPING:
125 g (4 oz) plain
  chocolate
2 tablespoons milk

Cream the fat and sugar together until light and fluffy. Add the flour and rice and stir until the mixture binds together. Knead until smooth.

Roll out to a square and press evenly into a shallow 20 cm (8 inch) square tin; prick well. Bake in a preheated moderate oven, 180°C (350°F), Gas Mark 4, for 30 minutes. Cool in the tin.

Place the filling ingredients in a pan and heat gently, stirring until dissolved. Bring slowly to the boil, then cook, stirring, for 5 to 7 minutes, until golden. Spread over the biscuit mixture and leave to set.

For the topping, place the chocolate and milk in a small pan and heat gently until melted. Spread over the biscuits and leave to set. Cut into squares to serve.

Makes 16

Mint Ice Cream Cornets

MINT ICE CREAM:
3 egg yolks
150 g (5 oz) caster
  sugar
300 ml (½ pint) milk
1 tablespoon gelatine,
  dissolved in
  3 tablespoons water
6 drops green food
  colouring
1 teaspoon
  peppermint essence
1 × 410 g (14.5 oz)
  can evaporated
  milk, chilled
TO SERVE:
14 ice cream cornets
7 chocolate flakes,
  halved

To make the ice cream: place the egg yolks and sugar in a heatproof bowl and beat until pale and creamy. Bring the milk almost to the boil, pour onto the egg mixture and mix thoroughly.

Place the bowl over a pan of simmering water and stir until thickened. Add the gelatine and stir until dissolved. Strain, allow to cool, then stir in the colouring and essence. Leave until just beginning to set.

Whisk the evaporated milk until thick, then whisk in the custard. Turn into a rigid freezerproof container, cover, seal and freeze until firm.

Transfer to the refrigerator 30 minutes before serving to soften. Scoop into the cornets and stick half a chocolate flake in each.
Makes 14

Toffee Apples

14 short wooden
  sticks or skewers
14 medium dessert
  apples
750 g (1½ lb)
  demerara sugar
75 g (3 oz) butter
2 teaspoons vinegar
175 ml (6 fl oz)
  water
2 tablespoons golden
  syrup

Push a stick firmly into the core of each apple.

Heat the remaining ingredients gently in a large heavy-based pan until the sugar has dissolved. Bring to the boil and boil for 5 minutes, without stirring, until 143°C (290°F) is registered on a sugar thermometer, or until a little mixture dropped into cold water forms a hard ball; brush the sides of the pan with a brush dipped in water occasionally during boiling, to prevent crystals forming. Remove from the heat and dip the pan immediately into cold water to stop the cooking.

Tilt the pan slightly and dip the apples one at a time into the mixture. Lift out and twirl over the pan once or twice until evenly coated with toffee. Place on an oiled baking sheet until the toffee has hardened.
Makes 14

Popcornets

8 tablespoons corn oil
125 g (4 oz) popcorn
  kernels
4 tablespoons clear
  honey

Heat 2 tablespoons oil in a large heavy-based pan over high heat. Add a quarter of the corn, cover and cook, shaking the pan constantly, until the kernels have popped. Remove from the heat, pour over 1 tablespoon of the honey and stir thoroughly until coated. Transfer to a bowl and repeat with remaining popcorn. Spoon into paper cornets to serve.
Makes 14
To make paper cornets: Cut 30 cm (12 inch) squares of paper. Fold in half diagonally and crease firmly. Turn the two creased points in to meet the third point and secure along the join with sticky tape.

47

BARBECUE PARTY

A barbecue party is more suited to lunch time than tea and is a wonderful way to entertain children aged about 8 to 12 for a summer birthday. Unfortunately, the weather cannot be controlled so do make alternative arrangements in case of rain.

Place the barbecue in a position where there is plenty of space so that the children can watch and join in the cooking. Light the barbecue about 45 minutes before you want to start cooking so that the charcoal is at the correct temperature. Build up the fire with more charcoal about 20 minutes before cooking. Wait until the charcoal is ash grey before starting.

You will need a surface for utensils, sauces and

food. Have at least one helper – so one person can cook and the other serve – and make sure there is always an adult around. With supervision the children can cook the sausages and drumsticks.

If you can borrow a second barbecue it will speed things up considerably. If you only have a small barbecue, half-cook the chicken and sausages in the kitchen and finish off over the barbecue to give them the charcoal flavour. The same applies to potatoes, but if you are not short of space these are delicious wrapped in foil and cooked directly in the charcoal. Make sure everyone has a little of everything at once, so cook half portions first, then cook the second half while they are eating; this also saves the food getting cold. If you have a barbecue that's divided into sections it's a good idea to have one section less hot so that you can keep cooked food warm until needed.

Cooking times depend on how well the coals are burning. Use the times given as a guide; the important thing is to keep turning the food.

Make the party table bright and attractive, in a buffet style so the children can help themselves to relishes, salads and drinks. Our menu is enough for 12 children.

Pitta Pockets

1 kg (2 lb) sausages
7 pitta breads,
    warmed

Place the sausages on the barbecue grid and cook for about 10 minutes, turning frequently, until well browned all over.

Cut the pitta breads in half and loosen inside with a knife to make a pocket. Place a sausage inside each pocket and spoon in some Sweet and Sour Sauce.
Makes 14

Sweet and Sour Sauce

2 small onions
2 small carrots
2 tablespoons oil
1 × 227 g (8 oz) can
    pineapple pieces
6 tablespoons malt
    vinegar
1 tablespoon
    Worcestershire
    sauce
1 tablespoon soy
    sauce
5 tablespoons clear
    honey
4 teaspoons cornflour
salt and pepper

Chop the onions and carrots finely. Heat the oil in a pan, add the onions and carrots and fry for 5 minutes, until softened. Pour the pineapple juice into the pan. Add the vinegar, sauces and honey and simmer for 15 minutes, stirring occasionally.

Blend the cornflour with 6 tablespoons water and stir into the sauce.

Add the pineapple, and salt and pepper to taste. Bring to the boil, stirring, then simmer for about 5 minutes until thickened.

Serve hot with Pitta Pockets, Barbecued Drumsticks and Spare Ribs.
Makes about 450 ml (¾ pint)

Barbecued Spare Ribs

2 kg (4½ lb) pork
    spare ribs
BARBECUE SAUCE:
2 teaspoons soy sauce
2 teaspoons Worcester-
    shire sauce
4 tablespoons tomato
    ketchup
2 tablespoons fruit
    sauce
2 teaspoons soft
    brown sugar
1 teaspoon French
    mustard

Mix the sauce ingredients together in a small basin.

Cut the ribs into serving pieces and brush with the sauce. Leave to marinate for 1 to 2 hours.

Place the ribs on the barbecue grid and cook for 5 to 10 minutes, turning frequently and basting with the remaining sauce, until crisp. Serve with Sweet and Sour Sauce.
Serves 12

Sweetcorn Salad

2 × 326 g (11½ oz)
  cans sweetcorn
2 sticks celery
4 tomatoes
4 spring onions
4 tablespoons
  mayonnaise
1 tablespoon French
  mustard

Drain the sweetcorn and place in a serving bowl. Chop the celery, tomatoes and spring onions finely and add to the bowl with the remaining ingredients. Toss thoroughly to serve.
Serves 12

Barbecued Potatoes

12 medium potatoes
oil for brushing
salt
butter to serve

Brush the potato skins with oil and sprinkle with salt. Slit each potato down one side.

If space on the barbecue is limited, bake the potatoes in a preheated moderately hot oven, 200°C (400°F), Gas Mark 6, for 45 minutes. Place the potatoes in the hot charcoal for a further 10 minutes.

If you have room on the barbecue, wrap potatoes in a double thickness of foil and cook in the charcoal for about 45 minutes, turning occasionally. Serve with butter.
Serves 12

Barbecued Drumsticks

12 chicken drumsticks
HONEY AND ORANGE
  SAUCE:
2 tablespoons clear
  honey
1 tablespoon Worcester-
  shire sauce
grated rind and juice
  of ½ orange
1 tablespoon tomato
  purée
1 tablespoon soy sauce

Mix the sauce ingredients together in a small basin and use to brush all over the drumsticks. Place them all on a large piece of foil and fold over to enclose completely. Leave to marinate for 1 hour.

Remove the foil, place the chicken on the barbecue grid and cook for 15 to 20 minutes, turning frequently and basting with the remaining sauce, until the skin is crisp. Serve with Sweet and Sour Sauce (page 50).
Serves 12

Apple and Ginger Fizz

*1.2 litres (2 pints)
  apple juice*
*600 ml (1 pint)
  ginger ale*
ice cubes
1 red-skinned apple

Place the apple juice and ginger ale in a jug. Add ice cubes. Thinly slice the apple, discarding the core. Float the apple slices on the drink.
Makes 1.75 litres (3 pints)

Giant Chocolate Chips

*125 g (4 oz) butter or
  margarine*
*50 g (2 oz) soft
  brown sugar*
1 egg, beaten
*150 g (5 oz) self-
  raising flour, sifted*
*175 g (6 oz) plain
  chocolate, finely
  chopped*
*50 g (2 oz) split
  almonds, chopped*

Beat the fat and sugar together until light and fluffy. Add the egg and beat thoroughly. Mix in the flour, chocolate and almonds.

Place 12 spoonfuls of the mixture well apart on greased baking sheets and spread each out to a 10 cm (4 inch) circle with a damp fork.

Bake in a preheated moderate oven, 180°C (350°F), Gas Mark 4, for 15 minutes, until golden. Leave on the baking sheets for 2 minutes, then transfer to a wire rack to cool.
Makes 12

Strawberry Milk Shake

350 g (12 oz)
    strawberries
2 tablespoons caster
    sugar
900 ml (1½ pints)
    milk
4 scoops vanilla ice
    cream

Place half the strawberries, sugar, milk and ice cream in an electric blender or food processor. Blend for 20 seconds. Pour into a jug. Repeat with remaining ingredients.
Serve with straws.
Makes 1.5 litres (2½ pints)

Chocolate Peanut Bars

125 g (4 oz) plain
    chocolate, chopped
75 g (3 oz) crunchy
    peanut butter
4 tablespoons golden
    syrup
1 tablespoon water
75 g (3 oz) unsalted
    peanuts, chopped
125 g (4 oz) bran
    flakes

Place the chocolate, peanut butter, syrup and water in a pan and heat gently until melted. Stir in the peanuts and bran flakes and mix thoroughly.
  Turn into a lined and greased 18 × 28 cm (7 × 11 inch) baking tin and smooth the surface. Chill in the refrigerator until set. Cut into bars to serve.
Makes 20

55

Toasted Marshmallows

2 packets marshmallows

Place 2 marshmallows on a long skewer. Hold over the barbecue, turning frequently until they puff up and turn golden. Serve immediately.
Serves 12

Baked Bananas

12 slightly under-ripe bananas

Bury the bananas, in their skins, in the charcoal embers just outside the hottest part of the fire. Leave for about 5 minutes, until the skins are charred. Remove from the fire with tongs.

Serve in a napkin or on a plate with a spoon. Peel back a strip of skin when cool enough to eat.
Serves 12

Rocky Road Cornets

3 egg yolks
75 g (3 oz) soft
  brown sugar
175 g (6 oz) plain
  chocolate, chopped
284 ml (½ pint)
  single cream
142 ml (5 fl oz)
  double cream
125 g (4 oz)
  marshmallows,
  each snipped into
  4 pieces
50 g (2 oz) split
  almonds, browned
  and chopped
12 ice cream cornets

Beat the egg yolks with the sugar in a heatproof bowl until creamy. Place the chocolate in a pan with the single cream and heat gently until melted. Bring just to the boil, then pour onto the egg yolk mixture and mix thoroughly. Place the bowl over a pan of simmering water and stir constantly until thickened. Strain and allow to cool.

Whip the double cream until it forms soft peaks, then fold in the chocolate custard. Pour into a rigid freezerproof container, cover and freeze for 2 to 3 hours until half-frozen. Stir well, then mix in the marshmallows and almonds. Return to the freezer and freeze until firm.

Transfer to the refrigerator 20 minutes before serving to soften, then scoop into the ice cream cornets.
Serves 12

DISCO PARTY

Older children love to feel grown-up and a larger party arranged at a later hour will be a special event in itself for 10- to 13-year-olds. Younger children, too – especially girls – might like the idea of a disco party. Hold it at an earlier time and change the menu to suit.

Older brothers and sisters are usually quite pleased to help with this sort of party, which makes your task easier. If you can, get an older teenager to arrange a disco dancing competition: she could first give a demonstration then judge the competitors.

Silver foil is invaluable for decorating the buffet table and room: cut it into strips and you can do all sorts of wonderful things with it. Your children will probably have great fun doing this.

Food is of secondary importance to the music – which must be loud and constant! Nevertheless, the guests will do justice to the efforts you make. Puddings are very popular, but don't prepare vast quantities of anything as much of the time will be spent dancing. Arrange the food on a table so that guests can help themselves when they want to. Keep it fairly simple, so it can be eaten with just fingers or forks.

This menu will serve about 20 children and most of it can be prepared in advance. Prepare the potatoes the day before and pop into the oven for 30 minutes to heat through and brown before serving. Cook the Devilled Chicken for 30 minutes early in the day, then brush with the sauces. Cook for a further 30 minutes to reheat just before required.

Cook the rice the day before and store in the refrigerator. Place in a roasting pan lined with buttered foil and stir in the vegetables. Cover with foil and heat through in a moderate oven 30 minutes before serving.

The Coffee Meringues and Chocolate Choux Buns can both be cooked in advance but finish during the afternoon of the party or they will become soggy.

The Record cake is intended for this party – easy to prepare and very effective.

Sausage and Bacon Kebabs

30 rashers streaky
   bacon, derinded
   and stretched
60 cocktail sausages
10 small onions, cut
   into wedges
4 tablespoons oil
salt and pepper

Cut each bacon rasher in half and roll up. Thread the bacon, sausage and onion alternately onto 20 skewers. Brush with oil and sprinkle with salt and pepper. Cook under a preheated hot grill for 3 to 4 minutes on each side. Serve hot.
Makes 20

Devilled Chicken

20 chicken thigh
   portions
2 tablespoons sugar
2 tablespoons salt
1 tablespoon ground
   ginger
1 tablespoon mustard
   powder
2 teaspoons curry
   powder
50 g (2 oz) butter
150 ml (¼ pint)
   tomato ketchup
1 tablespoon curry
   sauce
2 tablespoons soy
   sauce

Place the chicken portions on a board. Mix the sugar, salt, ginger, mustard and curry powder together. Rub well into the surface of the chicken. Leave for 2 hours.

Arrange the chicken on a grid in 2 roasting pans. Melt the butter and brush all over the chicken. Bake in a preheated moderately hot oven, 200°C (400°F), Gas Mark 6, for 30 minutes, until golden brown.

Mix the ketchup and sauces together and brush over the chicken portions. Return to the oven for 10 minutes. Arrange on a warmed serving dish and serve immediately.
Serves 20

Corn-Stuffed Potatoes

10 large potatoes
250 g (8 oz)
   Cheddar cheese,
   grated
125 g (4 oz) butter
2 tablespoons
   chopped parsley
4 tablespoons milk
salt and pepper
1 × 326 g (11½ oz)
   can sweetcorn,
   drained

Make a slit along one side of each potato and bake in a preheated moderately hot oven, 200°C (400°F), Gas Mark 6, for 1¼ hours or until cooked.

Halve the potatoes lengthways. Scoop out the flesh into a bowl and mash with half the cheese, the butter, parsley, milk, and salt and pepper to taste. Mix in the sweetcorn.

Spoon the mixture into the potato shells. Sprinkle with remaining cheese and return to the oven for 15 minutes or until golden. Serve hot.
Serves 20

Fried Rice with Almonds

3 tablespoons oil
2 onions, chopped
3 celery sticks, sliced
2 red peppers, cored,
    seeded and chopped
75 g (3 oz) flaked
    almonds
500 g (1 lb) long-
    grain rice, cooked
250 g (8 oz) frozen
    peas, cooked
salt and pepper

Heat the oil in a large pan, add the onions and fry until softened. Add the celery and red pepper and fry for 3 to 4 minutes. Add the almonds and fry for 2 minutes, until golden brown. Stir in the rice, peas, and salt and pepper to taste and heat through gently. Serve warm.

Serves 20

Coleslaw Salad

4 red dessert apples
1 head of celery
1 bunch spring onions
1.25 kg (2½ lb)
  white cabbage
175 g (6 oz) sultanas
DRESSING:
142 ml (5 fl oz)
  soured cream
juice of 1 lemon
2 teaspoons clear
  honey
300 ml (½ pint)
  mayonnaise
salt and pepper

Place the dressing ingredients in a bowl, with salt and pepper to taste, and mix together thoroughly.

Core and thinly slice the apple. Place in a salad bowl, pour over the dressing and mix well. Thinly slice the celery, chop the spring onions and shred the cabbage. Add to the bowl with the sultanas and toss thoroughly.

Serves 20

Apricot Cooler

1.2 litres (2 pints)
  orange juice
2 × 411 g (14½ oz)
  cans apricot halves
ice cubes
900 ml (1½ pints)
  lemonade
1 orange, thinly
  sliced

Place half the orange juice and apricots with their juice, in an electric blender or food processor. Blend on maximum speed for 1 minute. Repeat with remaining orange juice and apricots. Pour into 2 jugs and add the ice cubes.

Just before serving, pour over the lemonade. Top with orange slices.

Makes 3 litres (5½ pints)

Bean Sprout and Mushroom Salad

1 kg (2 lb) button
    mushrooms, sliced
750 g (1½ lb) bean
    sprouts
2 cartons mustard and
    cress
FRENCH DRESSING:
150 ml (¼ pint) oil
4 tablespoons red
    wine vinegar
1 teaspoon sugar
1 teaspoon French
    mustard
salt and pepper

Place the dressing ingredients in a screw top jar, with salt and pepper to taste, and shake well.

Place the mushrooms in a salad bowl and pour over the dressing. Toss well and leave to marinate for 1 hour. Just before serving, add the bean sprouts and mustard and cress and toss thoroughly.

Serves 20

NOTE: Use corn oil or a mixture of olive oil and corn oil for the dressing.

Fruit Punch

1.2 litres (2 pints)
    fruit cocktail drink
900 ml (1½ pints)
    apple juice
1.2 litres (2 pints)
    sweet cider
6 strawberries, sliced
1 apple, thinly sliced

Place half the fruit cocktail drink and half the apple juice in a jug and top up with cider. Place the remaining drinks in a second jug. Float the sliced fruit on top.

Makes 3 litres (5½ pints)

Banana Ice Cream with Butterscotch Sauce

2 × 410 g (14.5 oz)
cans evaporated
milk, chilled
300 g (10 oz) soft
brown sugar
6 ripe bananas
2 tablespoons lemon
juice
BUTTERSCOTCH
SAUCE:
284 ml (½ pint)
double cream
125 g (4 oz) unsalted
butter
175 g (6 oz) soft
brown sugar

Whisk the evaporated milk until thick and mousse-like, using an electric mixer if possible, then whisk in the sugar.

Mash the bananas to a pulp with the lemon juice, then whisk into the evaporated milk. Spoon into two 1 kg (2 lb) loaf tins, cover with foil and freeze until firm.

To make the sauce, place all the ingredients in a heavy-based pan. Heat gently, stirring until the sugar has dissolved, then bring to the boil and boil for 2 minutes, until syrupy.

Turn the ice cream onto a serving dish and place in the refrigerator 30 minutes before serving to soften. Cut into slices and pour over the hot or cold butterscotch sauce to serve.
Serves 20

Chocolate Choux Buns

4-egg quantity choux
pastry*
250 ml (8 fl oz)
double cream,
whipped
MINT CHOCOLATE
SAUCE:
15 wafer thin
chocolate mints
4 tablespoons single
cream

Place heaped tablespoons of the choux pastry well apart on dampened baking sheets. Bake in a preheated hot oven, 220°C (425°F), Gas Mark 7, for 10 minutes. Lower the temperature to 190°C (375°F), Gas Mark 5, and bake for 20 to 25 minutes, until crisp and golden brown. Make a slit in the side of each bun to allow the steam to escape and cool on a wire rack.

Using a piping bag fitted with a 1 cm (½ inch) fluted nozzle, pipe cream into each choux bun.

To make the sauce, place the chocolate mints and cream in a small heatproof bowl over a pan of simmering water. When the chocolate has melted, stir until the sauce is smooth. Spoon a little sauce over each bun and leave to set.
Makes 20

Coffee Meringues

350 g (12 oz) caster
   sugar
2 tablespoons instant
   coffee powder
6 egg whites
250 ml (8 fl oz)
   double cream,
   whipped

Sift the caster sugar and coffee powder together. Whisk the egg whites until stiff and dry-looking, then gradually whisk in a quarter of the sugar mixture. Carefully fold in the remainder with a metal spoon.

Put the mixture into a piping bag fitted with a 1 cm (½ inch) plain nozzle. Pipe into mounds on a baking sheet lined with silicone paper.

Bake in a preheated very cool oven, 110°C (225°F), Gas Mark ¼, for 2 hours, until crisp. Cool on a wire rack, then remove the paper.

Sandwich the meringues together in pairs with the cream to serve.
Makes 20 to 24

TEENAGE PARTY

A teenager will choose to hold a party in the evening and a buffet-style supper is the easiest to manage for a larger group. Remove as much furniture as possible, leaving a central space for dancing. Place the buffet table against a wall and cover completely with a sheet.

A theme party is popular with this age group. Colours are easy themes to follow through: for example, a black and white evening or a purple party. Music is essential, of course. A certain amount of supervision and unobtrusive assistance is advisable during the serving of the food, but then a discreet disappearance will be appreciated. However, in return for your disappearing act, they should clear up their own mess at the end of the evening!

Two alternative menus are provided for this party. Both are sufficient to serve 20 people. The hot menu comprises moussaka, chicken à la king – served with rice and a crisp green salad – followed by caramel ice cream and meringue baskets. A cider cup accompanies the buffet.

The alternative menu consists of pizza, quiche, potato and dill mayonnaise, Chinese cabbage salad and garlic bread, with chocolate ice cream caramel cake and marshmallow mousse to follow. Ruby punch is the drink for this menu.

Most of the suggested dishes in these two menus can be prepared and frozen in advance, including the pizza, the quiche pastry cases and the moussaka without its sauce. The latter dishes can be finished on the day. All of the desserts freeze well, but the meringue baskets are best filled on the day.

Moussaka

1.5 kg (3 lb)
 aubergines, sliced
salt and pepper
300 ml (½ pint) corn
 oil
6 onions, chopped
1.5 kg (3 lb) lamb,
 minced
3 cloves garlic,
 crushed
3 tablespoons tomato
 purée
3 × 397 g (14 oz)
 cans tomatoes
1.5 kg (3 lb)
 potatoes, parboiled
 and thickly sliced
SAUCE:
75 g (3 oz) butter or
 margarine
75 g (3 oz) plain
 flour
900 ml (1½ pints)
 milk
3 egg yolks
125 g (4 oz)
 Cheddar cheese,
 grated

Sprinkle the aubergines with salt and leave for 30 minutes. Drain and dry with kitchen paper.

Heat some of the oil in 2 large frying pans and fry the aubergines in batches until golden, adding more oil as necessary. Remove and set aside.

Add a little more oil to the pans, and fry the onions until soft. Add the meat and garlic and fry briskly, stirring, for 10 minutes. Drain off excess fat. Add 1 teaspoon salt, and pepper to taste, to each pan. Stir in the tomato purée and tomatoes, with their juice. Bring to the boil and simmer for 30 minutes.

Layer the aubergines, meat mixture and potatoes in 3 casseroles, finishing with aubergines.

To make the sauce, melt the fat in a pan and stir in the flour. Gradually stir in the milk and cook, stirring, until thickened. Remove from the heat and stir in the egg yolks, and salt and pepper to taste. Pour over the aubergines and sprinkle with cheese.

Bake in a preheated moderately hot oven, 200°C (400°F), Gas Mark 6, for 10 to 15 minutes, until golden brown. Serve with a crisp green salad.
Serves 20

Chicken à la King

150 ml (¼ pint) oil
4 onions, chopped
3 green peppers, cored,
    seeded and diced
3 red peppers, cored,
    seeded and diced
750 g (1½ lb) button
    mushrooms,
    quartered
125 g (4 oz) plain
    flour
300 ml (½ pint) milk
1.2 litres (2 pints)
    chicken stock
1.5 kg (3 lb) cooked
    chicken, diced
1 teaspoon paprika
salt
142 ml (¼ pint)
    single cream
1 tablespoon lemon
    juice

Heat the oil in a large pan, add the onions and diced peppers and fry until softened. Add the mushrooms and cook, stirring for 2 minutes. Stir in the flour and cook for 1 minute, then gradually stir in the milk. Bring to the boil, stirring.

Add the stock and simmer for 3 minutes, until thickened. Add the chicken, paprika, and salt to taste. Simmer for 5 minutes until heated through.

Remove from the heat and stir in the cream and lemon juice. Serve immediately, with plain boiled rice.

Serves 20

NOTE: You will need 750 g (1½ lb) rice for this quantity of chicken. The rice can be cooked before the chicken and kept warm in buttered foil in a moderate oven for 30 minutes.

Cider Cup

2.25 litres (4 pints)
  medium sweet cider
300 ml (½ pint)
  undiluted orange
  squash
150 ml (¼ pint) sweet
  sherry (optional)
1 red dessert apple
1.2 litres (2 pints)
  soda water
ice cubes

Place the cider, squash and sherry if using, in a punch bowl. Slice the apple thinly, discarding the core, and add to the bowl.

Just before serving, add the soda water and ice cubes.

Makes 3.75 litres (6¾ pints)

Caramel Ice Cream

175 g (6 oz)
  granulated sugar
4 tablespoons cold
  water
90 ml (3 fl oz)
  boiling water
6 egg yolks, beaten
900 ml (1½ pints)
  single cream
4 egg whites
125 g (4 oz) soft
  brown sugar
284 ml (½ pint)
  double cream,
  lightly whipped
CHOCOLATE SAUCE:
175 g (6 oz) plain
  chocolate, chopped
50 g (2 oz) caster
  sugar
250 ml (8 fl oz) milk

Place the granulated sugar and cold water in a heavy-based pan and heat very gently until dissolved. Increase the heat and boil until it turns a rich nut brown colour.

Carefully pour in the boiling water and stir until the caramel has melted. Cool, then beat into the egg yolks. Return to the pan, add half the single cream and heat gently, stirring, until the mixture coats the back of a wooden spoon. Stir in the remaining single cream and allow to cool.

Whisk the egg whites until soft peaks form, then whisk in the brown sugar a little at a time. Continue whisking until stiff. Fold the caramel mixture into the whipped double cream, then into the meringue. Pour into a rigid freezerproof container and freeze until firm.

To make the chocolate sauce, place all the ingredients in a small pan and heat gently, stirring, until the sugar has dissolved. Simmer for 2 to 3 minutes. Cool, if preferred.

Transfer the ice cream to the refrigerator 30 minutes before serving to soften. Scoop into chilled dishes and pour on the chocolate sauce to serve.

Serves 20

Meringue Baskets

8 egg whites
½ teaspoon vanilla
   essence
500 g (1 lb) caster
   sugar
FILLING:
284 ml (½ pint)
   whipping cream,
   whipped
350 g (12 oz)
   strawberries or
   raspberries
icing sugar, sifted

Put 4 egg whites in a heatproof bowl and whisk until stiff. Place over a pan of simmering water and whisk in half the vanilla. Whisk in half the sugar, a tablespoon at a time, until stiff.

Line a baking sheet with silicone paper and draw on ten 6 cm (2½ inch) circles. Spread half the meringue over the circles. Put the remaining meringue into a piping bag fitted with a 5 mm (¼ inch) fluted nozzle and pipe round the edge of each base. Repeat with remaining meringue ingredients to make 20 baskets.

Bake in a preheated cool oven, 150°C (300°F), Gas Mark 2, for 1 to 1¼ hours. Cool on a wire rack; remove the paper.

Spoon a little cream into each basket and arrange the fruit on top. Sprinkle with icing sugar to serve.
Makes 20

Pizza

DOUGH:
500 g (1 lb) plain
  flour
1 teaspoon salt
7 g (1/4 oz) dried
  yeast
1 teaspoon sugar
300 ml (1/2 pint)
  warm water
2 tablespoons oil
TOPPING:
3 tablespoons oil
3 large onions,
  chopped
3 × 397 g (14 oz) cans
  tomatoes, drained
  and chopped
2 teaspoons dried
  oregano
salt and pepper
3 tablespoons tomato
  purée
500 g (1 lb)
  Mozzarella cheese,
  thinly sliced
2 × 50 g (1¾ oz)
  cans anchovy
  fillets, drained and
  halved lengthways
18 black olives,
  halved and stoned

Sift the flour and salt together into a
bowl. Dissolve the yeast and sugar in
a little of the water and leave in a
warm place for 10 minutes. Add to
the flour with the remaining water
and the oil. Mix to a soft dough.

Turn onto a floured surface and
knead for 10 minutes, until smooth
and elastic. Place in a clean bowl,
cover and leave to rise in a warm
place for about 1½ hours, until
doubled in size.

For the topping, heat the oil in a
pan, add the onions and fry until
softened. Add the tomatoes, oregano,
and salt and pepper to taste; cook for
5 minutes. Leave to cool.

Turn the dough onto a floured
surface and knead for a few minutes.
Divide into 3 pieces, roll each into a
25 cm (10 inch) circle and place on
greased baking sheets. Spread
1 tablespoon tomato purée over each
dough round. Divide the tomato
mixture between the rounds and
cover with cheese. Arrange the
anchovies and olives on top.

Bake in a preheated moderately hot
oven, 200°C (400°F), Gas Mark 6, for
15 to 20 minutes. Serve immediately.
Serves 18 to 24

Potato and Dill Mayonnaise

1.75 kg (4 lb) new
  potatoes
salt
4 tablespoons French
  dressing
6-8 spring onions
4 dill cucumbers
300 ml (1/2 pint)
  mayonnaise
4 tablespoons natural
  yogurt

Cook the potatoes in their skins in
boiling salted water for about
15 minutes, until just tender. Drain and
remove the skins. Cut into large dice
and place in a bowl. Add the French
dressing, toss lightly and leave to
cool. Slice the onions and cucumber
thinly and add to the potatoes.

Mix the mayonnaise and yogurt
until smooth. Add to the salad and
toss well. Transfer to bowls to serve.
Serves 20

Garlic Bread

1 large French loaf
175 g (6 oz) butter,
    softened
2 cloves garlic,
    crushed
1 tablespoon chopped
    parsley
salt and pepper

Make diagonal cuts 2.5 cm (1 inch) apart three-quarters of the way through the French loaf. Cream together the butter, garlic, parsley, and salt and pepper to taste until thoroughly mixed. Spread liberally between the slices; spread any remaining butter over the top.

Wrap in foil and bake in a preheated moderately hot oven, 200°C (400°F), Gas Mark 6, for 10 minutes. Draw the foil back to expose the top of the loaf and cook for a further 5 to 10 minutes, until crisp. Remove the foil, cut through each slice and serve hot.
Serves 20

Cheese and Onion Quiche

CHEESE PASTRY:
*500 g (1 lb) plain
   flour*
½ teaspoon salt
*1 teaspoon dry
   mustard*
*250 g (8 oz) butter or
   margarine*
*250 g (8 oz) Cheddar
   cheese, grated*
*6 tablespoons water
   (approximately)*

FILLING:
6 tablespoons oil
6 onions, chopped
9 eggs
600 ml (1 pint) milk
*750 g (1½ lb) Cheddar
   cheese, grated*
*3 tablespoons
   chopped parsley*
salt and pepper

Sift the flour, salt and mustard into a
bowl. Rub in the fat until the mixture
resembles breadcrumbs, then stir in
the cheese. Add the water gradually
and mix to a firm dough. Turn onto a
floured surface and knead lightly.

Divide the dough into 3 pieces, roll
out and use to line three 23 cm (9 inch)
flan tins. Chill for 15 minutes while
making the filling.

Heat the oil in a pan, add the
onions and fry gently until
transparent. Beat the eggs and milk
together in a large bowl, then stir in
the cheese, onions, parsley, and salt
and pepper to taste.

Divide between the pastry cases
and bake in a preheated moderately
hot oven, 190°C (375°F), Gas Mark 5,
for 35 minutes, until golden and set.
Serve hot or cold.
Serves 18 to 24

74

Chinese Cabbage Salad

2 small Chinese
   cabbages, shredded
500 g (1 lb) bean
   sprouts
2 bunches watercress
1 apple, sliced
2 avocado pears
VINAIGRETTE
   DRESSING:
150 ml (¼ pint)
   olive oil
4 tablespoons wine
   vinegar
1 teaspoon sugar
1 teaspoon French
   mustard
2 tablespoons chopped
   mixed herbs
   (mint, parsley,
   chives, thyme)

Place the cabbage and bean sprouts in a salad bowl. Separate the watercress into sprigs; add to bowl with the apple.

Place the dressing ingredients in a screw-topped jar and shake well. Peel the avocado pears and slice them into another bowl. Pour over the dressing to coat. Add to the remaining salad and toss well before serving.

Serves 20

Ruby Punch

350 ml (12 fl oz)
  blackcurrant health
  drink
150 ml (¼ pint)
  sweet sherry
  (optional)
2.5 litres (4½ pints)
  soda water
1 lemon, thinly sliced

Place the blackcurrant juice and sherry, if using, in a jug. Pour on the soda water and float the lemon slices on top.

Makes about 2.75 litres (5 pints)

Chocolate Caramel Ice Cream Cake

125 g (4 oz) plain
  flour
50 g (2 oz) cocoa
  powder
6 eggs
275 g (9 oz) caster
  sugar
1 quantity Caramel
  Ice Cream (see
  page 70)
284 ml (½ pint)
  double cream,
  whipped
25 g (1 oz) plain
  chocolate, melted

Sift the flour and cocoa together and set aside. Place the eggs and sugar in a large bowl and whisk until the mixture is pale and thick enough to leave a trail. Carefully fold in the flour mixture, using a metal spoon.

Divide the mixture between two lined, greased and floured 23 cm (9 inch) cake tins and bake in a preheated moderately hot oven, 190°C (375°F), Gas Mark 5, for 20 to 25 minutes, until the cakes spring back when lightly pressed. Turn onto a wire rack to cool.

Remove the caramel ice cream from the freezer about 45 minutes before serving to soften.

Split the cakes in half horizontally. Spoon the softened ice cream onto the bottom half of each, spreading the softest ice cream near the edges, and smooth the top. Cover with the remaining sponge halves and smooth the ice cream round the centre.

Cover the tops of the cakes with the cream and pipe a border round the edges.

Place the melted chocolate in a greaseproof piping bag, snip off the end and pipe 'Happy Birthday' on one cake and the name on the other.

Serves 24

Marshmallow Mousse

2 raspberry jellies
300 ml (½ pint)
  boiling water
250 g (8 oz)
  marshmallows
2 × 410 g (14.5 oz)
  cans evaporated
  milk, chilled
284 ml (½ pint)
  whipping cream,
  whipped
250 g (8 oz)
  raspberries
  (optional)

Dissolve the jellies in the boiling
water. Leave until cool but not set.
Set aside 8 marshmallows; snip the
remainder into small pieces.

Whisk the evaporated milk until
thick, then whisk in the jelly. Fold in
the whipping cream, cut
marshmallows and raspberries if
using. Turn into two glass bowls and
chill until set.

Decorate with the reserved
marshmallows, halved, to serve.
Serves 20

77

NOVELTY CAKES

The birthday cake is the most important part of the party and for most children what it represents is far more important than how beautifully it is iced! Don't leave a novelty cake until the last minute and try to do it in a rush – it's a fiddly task and requires patience.

A Victoria sandwich is the easiest type of cake to work with. If possible, make it well in advance, leave it for a day before cutting to shape – so that it is not too crumbly – then freeze in a rigid container. Leave to thaw for 3 to 4 hours and ice it the day before the party. It is not advisable to freeze the completed cake.

Colourings, paint brushes, piping bags and nozzles will be needed, while liquorice allsorts are invaluable for all the little extras that cannot be made out of cake.

Hallowe'en Cake

3-egg Victoria
   sandwich cake
   mixture*
3 tablespoons apricot
   glaze*
350 g (12 oz) blue
   moulding icing*
50 g (2 oz)
   marzipan, thinly
   rolled
black food colouring
2-3 teaspoons apricot
   jam

Turn the cake mixture into a greased and lined 1.5 litre (2½ pint) ovenproof basin and level the surface. Bake in a preheated moderate oven, 160°C (325°F), Gas Mark 3, for 1 to 1¼ hours. Remove carefully and cool on a wire rack. Brush with apricot glaze.

Roll out the moulding icing thinly into a circle. Lift onto a rolling pin and position over the cake. Mould to the cake; cut off the excess and reserve. Place on a cake board.

Cut stars and crescent moons from the marzipan; paint some black. Stick the shapes onto the cake with jam. Mould a cat from the remaining moulding icing, paint with black colouring and allow to dry. Position on the cake. Arrange candles around the edge if desired.

Makes one Hallowe'en cake

Pirate Galleon

3-egg chocolate
  Victoria sandwich
  cake mixture*
350 g (12 oz) coffee
  butter icing*
6-8 ice cream wafers
1 sheet of rice paper
3 drinking straws
50 g (2 oz) brown
  glacé icing*
1 sweet cigarette
red food colouring
1 liquorice allsort
8 liquorice comfits
2 polo mints

diagram 1

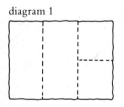

diagram 2

diagram 3

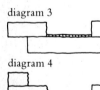

diagram 4

Line and grease a 20 × 30 cm (8 × 12 inch) Swiss roll tin. Turn the cake mixture into the tin and bake in a preheated moderate oven, 180°C (350°F), Gas Mark 4, for 20 to 25 minutes. Cool on a wire rack.

Cut the cake into 3 equal pieces; cut one piece in half and set aside (see diagram 1). Sandwich the two larger pieces together with butter icing. Cut to shape (see diagram 2); stick the 2 pieces cut from the bow end together with butter icing to form a triangle.

Cover the cake and bow piece with butter icing. Place the cake on a board and position the bow piece on the bow. Place 2 wafers behind for decking.

Cover one of the remaining pieces of sponge with icing and place on the stern for the first deck (see diagram 3).

Halve the remaining piece of cake, cover one half with icing and place on top and to the rear of the first deck (see diagram 4); discard the other piece. Place a wafer on each deck at the stern.

Cut sails from the rice paper and thread onto the straws. Using the brown glacé icing, pipe a skull and cross bones on 1 sail. Press the masts and sails in position, securing the front sail with a sweet cigarette.

Cut the remaining wafers into strips and position as railings, ledges and windows all round the ship. Press 1 strip into the side for a plank.

Colour the remaining butter icing red. Decorate the ship with piped red dots and piped brown scrolls. Cut an anchor from a liquorice allsort.

Cut comfits in half and press the rounded ends into the icing along the sides for cannons. Position polos and comfits as guns at the stern.

Makes one pirate galleon

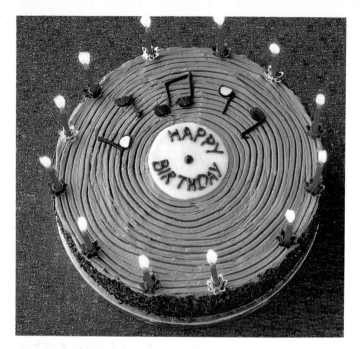

Record Cake

5-egg Victoria
    sandwich cake
    mixture*
250 g (8 oz)
    chocolate butter
    icing*
chocolate sugar
    strands
50 g (2 oz) glacé
    icing*
brown food colouring
black and white
    liquorice allsorts,
    cut into strips and
    circles

Turn the cake mixture into a 25 cm
(10 inch) cake tin and bake in a
preheated moderate oven, 160°C
(325°F), Gas Mark 3, for 55 to
60 minutes. Cool on a wire rack.

Split the cake into two layers and
sandwich together with a third of the
butter icing. Spread another third
round the side of the cake and coat
with sugar strands. Place on a board.

Spread the remaining butter icing
on top and mark a circular grooved
pattern using a fork, leaving a smooth
circle in the centre. Fill this with two
thirds of the glacé icing. Leave to set.

Arrange the liquorice pieces on the
cake to represent notes. Colour the
remaining glacé icing brown, spoon
into a greaseproof piping bag fitted
with a No 2 writing nozzle and write
'Happy Birthday' on the cake. Put
candles around the edge if desired.
Makes one record cake

Post Box

2-egg Victoria
  sandwich cake
  mixture*
3 tablespoons apricot
  glaze*
250 g (8 oz) red
  moulding icing*
1 large round biscuit
2-3 pieces of liquorice
  ribbon
25 g (1 oz) black or
  brown glacé icing*
1 liquorice allsort
icing sugar, sifted
1 robin (optional)

Cleanly remove one end from 2 empty 397 g (14 oz) cans. Clean the cans thoroughly, then grease and flour them. Two-thirds fill the cans with the cake mixture and bake in a preheated moderate oven, 160°C (325°F), Gas Mark 3, for 30 to 35 minutes. Loosen the cakes round the edge with a long thin knife, then turn out and cool on a wire rack.

Cut the rounded tops off the cakes and discard. Cut a 2.5 cm (1 inch) piece from one cake, shape into a dome and set aside. Sandwich the 2 cakes together with apricot glaze, then brush all over with glaze.

Roll out three quarters of the moulding icing thinly on a surface sprinkled with cornflour, to an oblong measuring 25 × 15 cm (10 × 6 inches) and trim the edges; reserve trimmings. Wrap icing round the cake and mould the join together with a palette knife.

Stick the shaped dome onto the biscuit with a little apricot glaze and brush with glaze. Roll out remaining icing into a 13 cm (5 inch) circle and use to cover the dome and biscuit. Place on top of the cake to form the post box top. Make ridges round the top, using the back of a knife.

Fix 2 pieces of liquorice ribbon around the base of the post box with glaze. Press a strip of liquorice ribbon in position near the top for the opening. Cut a lid for the opening from the moulding icing trimmings and press into position. Fix a liquorice allsort below the opening to represent the 'collection times' label. Pipe on a door and writing, using glacé icing.

Sprinkle with icing sugar to represent snow and position the robin on top, if using.

Makes one post box

Illustrated on page 85

Mushroom House

4-egg Victoria
  sandwich cake
  mixture*
75 g (3 oz) chocolate
  butter icing*
3 tablespoons apricot
  glaze*
250 g (8 oz) red
  moulding icing*
liquorice allsorts
25 g (1 oz) green
  butter icing*
1 marshmallow
hundreds and
  thousands
sugar flowers

Cleanly remove one end from an empty 793 g (1 lb 12 oz) can and clean the can thoroughly. Grease and flour the can and a 1.2 litre (2 pint) ovenproof bowl. Turn the cake mixture into the containers, two-thirds filling the can. Level the surfaces.

Bake in a preheated moderate oven, 160°C (325°F), Gas Mark 3, for 50 minutes for the can and 55 to 60 minutes for the basin. Loosen round the edges with a long thin knife and turn out onto a wire rack to cool.

Cover the 'can' cake with chocolate butter icing, reserving 2 tablespoons, and place on a cake board. Brush the 'basin' cake with apricot glaze. Roll out the moulding icing thinly on a surface sprinkled with cornflour into a 28 cm (11 inch) circle. Lift onto a rolling pin and position over the basin cake. Mould to the cake, folding any excess underneath at the base. Carefully place this cake on top of the other one for the roof.

Cut liquorice allsorts into thin slices and stick onto the roof with a little glaze to make spots.

Make doors and windows from liquorice allsorts and a chimney from a black liquorice allsort and a marshmallow. Press into position. Use the reserved butter icing to pipe on window frames and door knobs.

Ice the board with green butter icing and rough up with a fork to represent grass. Make a path up to the door with small triangles of liquorice and hundreds and thousands. Decorate with sugar flowers.

Makes one mushroom house

Christmas Tree

4-egg Victoria
    sandwich cake
    mixture*
375 g (12 oz) butter
    icing*
125 g (4 oz) apricot
    glaze*
red, yellow and green
    food colourings
1 star, cut from
    marzipan
silver balls
smarties
liquorice comfits
candles in holders

Turn the cake mixture into two 20 ×
30 cm (8 × 12 inch) Swiss roll tins.
Bake in a preheated moderate oven,
180°C (350°F), Gas Mark 4, for 20 to
25 minutes; cool on a wire rack.

Sandwich the cakes together with a
quarter of the icing. Cut to tree shape
(see diagram) attaching 2 cut out
pieces to the top. Stick 2 other cut
pieces together with a little icing and
shape to form the tub.

Brush cut edges with apricot glaze
and leave to dry. Colour one quarter
of the icing red, 2 tablespoons yellow
and the remainder green. Spread the
green icing over the tree, then fork up.

Spread the red icing over the tub,
attach to the tree and pipe yellow
rosettes around the tub. Stick on the
star, silver balls, sweets and candles.
Makes one Christmas tree

Stable

3-egg Victoria
  sandwich cake
  mixture*
350 g (12 oz) butter
  icing*
1 packet ice cream
  wafers
16 wafer-thin
  chocolate mints
liquorice ribbon
green food colouring
1 packet sweet
  cigarettes
1 small Milky Way
  bar
2 Rolos
few pieces of vanilla
  fudge
sugar flowers

diagram 1

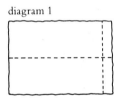

diagram 2

diagram 3

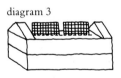

Turn the cake mixture into an 18 × 28 cm (7 × 11 inch) baking tin. Bake in a preheated moderate oven, 160°C (325°F), Gas Mark 3, for 30 to 35 minutes. Cool on a wire rack.

Cut the cake in half lengthways and cut off 2 cm (¾ inch) from one end of each piece (see diagram 1). Shape the 2 small pieces (as shown in diagram 2) to form gable ends.

Sandwich together the 2 slabs of cake with icing. Make a 1 cm (½ inch) deep cut along the centre of the cake.

Cover the cake completely with icing and place on a cake board. Place the gable ends in position and cover with icing.

Gently push 2 wafers vertically into the centre cut on the cake to come level with the tops of the gables (see diagram 3). Spread a little icing along the top edge of the wafers.

Position the chocolate mints at an angle from the edge of the cake to the tops of the wafers to form the roof.

Shape wafers to make doors and windows and press into position. Place a piece of liquorice ribbon at each end to represent drainpipes.

Colour the remaining icing green and spread thickly over the cake board. Place sweet cigarettes into the icing at intervals around the edge of the cake board, then stick thin strips of wafer onto them with a little icing to form fencing.

Remove the centre from the base of the Milky Way and fill with green icing to represent a trough. Place the Rolos together to form a barrel and place under the drain pipe. Mark the fudge with a fork and use to represent straw bales. Decorate with a few sugar flowers, and plastic animals if liked.

Makes one stable

Illustrated on page 89

Engine Cake

3-egg chocolate
  Victoria sandwich
  cake mixture*
250 g (8 oz)
  chocolate butter
  icing*
liquorice allsorts
4 iced biscuits
2 plain biscuits,
  halved
50 g (2 oz) yellow
  butter icing*
liquorice strips
hundreds and
  thousands

diagram 1

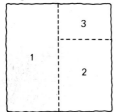

diagram 2

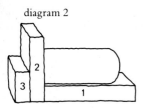

Line and grease an 18 cm (7 inch) square cake tin. Remove one end from an empty 397 g (14 oz) can, clean the can thoroughly, then grease and flour.

Turn the cake mixture into the prepared tins, only two-thirds filling the can. Bake in a preheated moderate oven, 160°C (325°F), Gas Mark 3, for 40 minutes for the cake tin and 45 to 50 minutes for the can. Turn onto a wire rack to cool, loosening the cake in the can with a long knife.

Following diagrams 1 and 2, cut the large cake in half and lay one piece on a cake board to form the base. Cut two thirds from the remaining half and place upright, cut side down, at one end of the base. Take the remaining third and place upright, cut side down, on the board beside the other two pieces.

Cover all the pieces, and the round cake, with chocolate butter icing. Place the round cake on the base to form the boiler section (see diagram 2). Neaten the icing.

Position 2 iced biscuits on each side for wheels. Cover the top halves of these with plain biscuit halves. Using liquorice allsorts, make the small wheels, lights, funnels and buffers; place in position.

Using the yellow icing and a No 3 writing nozzle, pipe along the edges of the engine and around the front of the boiler section. Pipe a handrail along the length of the engine and wheel arches on the halved biscuits.

Use liquorice allsorts, to make windows, coal and a face on the engine. Position liquorice strips and hundreds and thousands for the track. Add candles if desired.

Makes one engine

Helicopter

3-egg Victoria
  sandwich cake
  mixture*
250 g (8 oz) butter
  icing*
4 tablespoons apricot
  glaze*
250 g (8 oz)
  moulding icing*
green and brown food
  colourings
1 stick of rock, 2 cm
  (¾ inch) thick
5 ice cream cornets
2 ice cream wafers
liquorice allsorts
4 sweet lollipops
50 g (2 oz) brown
  glacé icing*
smarties

diagram 1

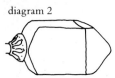

diagram 2

diagram 3

Line and grease two 500 g (1 lb) loaf tins. Turn the cake mixture into the tins and bake in a preheated moderate oven, 160°C (325°F), Gas Mark 3, for 1 hour. Cool on a wire rack.

Cut off the rounded tops and discard. Sandwich the cut surfaces together with butter icing. Cut 2 diagonal slices off the corners at one end and make a small, deep hole in the opposite end to hold the rock (see diagram 1).

Brush the shaped end with apricot glaze. Roll out the moulding icing thinly, lay over the glazed end and mould to represent the cockpit.

Colour the remaining butter icing green and spread over the rear of the helicopter, reserving 3 tablespoons icing. Paint areas with brown food colouring to resemble camouflage.

Insert the rock into the hole. Cut the cone ends from the cornets and discard all but one. Push one of the cornets, wide end first, over the rock up to the cake to form the tail plane (see diagram 2).

Cut 1 wafer lengthways into 4 strips to make blades. Shape one end of each into a point. Sandwich 2 liquorice allsorts together with butter icing. Spread a little butter icing on the top sweet and rest the blades on top with 4 points meeting at the centre. Place a little icing on 2 similar sweets and press down firmly on top of the blades. Set aside.

For the undercarriage you may need help. Push the remaining cornets along the lolly sticks, wide end first (see diagram 3). Holding the cake up with a fish slice, push the lolly sticks into the cake, one at each corner, so the smaller end of the cornet touches the cake (see diagram 4). Lower gently on to the 'pad' (cakeboard).

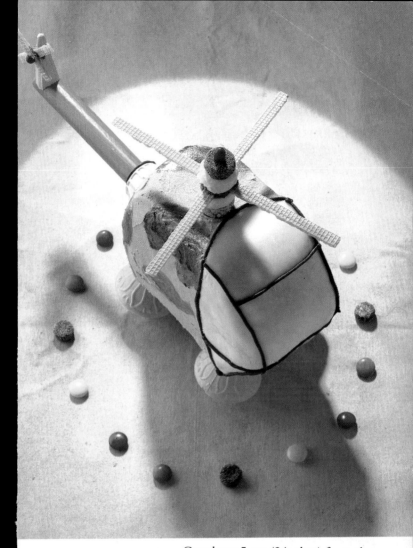

diagram 4

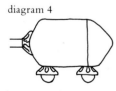

diagram 5

Cut about 5 cm (2 inches) from the end of the reserved cone. Cut 2 short wafer strips and stick diagonally with butter icing make the rear rotor blades. Fix to pointed end of the cone with butter icing and stick half a liquorice comfit in the centre (see diagram 5). Secure the cone to the end of the rock with butter icing. Fix the top rotor blade in position with butter icing and stick the other comfit half on top.

Use glacé icing to pipe on windows. Use smarties to mark the helicopter pad.
Makes one helicopter

BASIC RECIPES

For quantities different from those given here, simply increase or decrease the ingredients in proportion.

Victoria Sandwich Cake Mixture

250 g (8 oz) butter or margarine
250 g (8 oz) caster sugar
4 eggs
250 g (8 oz) self-raising flour, sifted
2 tablespoons hot water

Cream the fat and sugar together until light and fluffy. Beat in the eggs one at a time, adding a tablespoon of the flour with the second egg. Fold in the remaining flour with a metal spoon, then the hot water.

Turn the mixture into the prepared tin(s) and bake as directed, until the cakes spring back when lightly pressed.

Makes a 4-egg quantity

VARIATION

Chocolate: Blend 1 tablespoon cocoa powder with 2 tablespoons hot water. Cool slightly then beat in with the fat and sugar.

Choux Pastry

50 g (2 oz) butter or margarine
150 ml (¼ pint) water
65 g (2½ oz) plain flour, sifted
2 eggs, beaten

Melt the fat in a small pan, add the water and bring to the boil. Add the flour all at once and beat until the mixture leaves the sides of the pan. Cool, then add the eggs a little at a time, beating vigorously. Use as required.

Makes a 2-egg quantity

Shortcrust Pastry

125 g (4 oz) plain flour
50 g (2 oz) butter or margarine
1 tablespoon iced water

Sift the flour into a bowl. Rub in the butter or margarine until the mixture resembles fine breadcrumbs. Add the water gradually and mix to a firm dough. Use as required.

Makes a 125 g (4 oz) quantity

Apricot Glaze

125 g (4 oz) apricot
  jam
2 tablespoons water
squeeze of lemon
  juice

Heat the jam and water in a small pan gently until dissolved. Add the lemon juice, then sieve and return to the pan. Simmer until syrupy. Use warm.
Makes 125 g (4 oz)

Glacé Icing

125 g (4 oz) icing
  sugar
1 tablespoon warm
  water (approx)
few drops of food
  colouring (optional)

Sift the icing sugar into a mixing bowl and gradually stir in the water. The icing should be thick enough to coat the back of the spoon thickly. Beat in any colouring; use immediately.
Makes a 125 g (4 oz) quantity

Butter Icing

125 g (4 oz) butter
250 g (8 oz) icing
  sugar, sifted
2 tablespoons milk
flavouring (see below)
  or few drops of food
  colouring (optional)

Beat the butter with half the icing sugar until smooth. Beat in the remaining icing sugar with the milk and flavouring or colouring if using.
Makes a 250 g (8 oz) quantity
FLAVOURINGS
Chocolate: Blend 2 tablespoons cocoa powder with 2 tablespoons boiling water. Cool, then add to the mixture with only 1 tablespoon milk.
Coffee: Replace 1 tablespoon milk with 1 tablespoon coffee essence.

Moulding Icing

1 small egg white
1 rounded tablespoon
  liquid glucose
350 g (12 oz) icing
  sugar, sifted
  (approximately)
few drops of food
  colouring (optional)

Mix the egg white and glucose in a basin. Gradually add enough icing sugar to form a stiff paste. Turn onto a surface sprinkled with cornflour and knead until smooth. Wrap in cling film to prevent drying.

Before moulding icing is applied, the cake must be brushed with apricot glaze. Mould the icing to the cake by rubbing the surface with a circular movement, keeping hands dusted with icing sugar. Work any surplus icing to bottom of the cake and cut off; this can be used again.
Makes a 350 g (12 oz) quantity

INDEX

The merchant was hungry and decided that he would first take his horse to the stable. Then he would return and, if there was still no one in the room, he would have a good meal.

When he returned from the stable, the room was still empty so he sat down and enjoyed the supper.

After supper, Beauty's father felt sleepy and, crossing the hall, he found a bedroom all ready for use. He went to bed and slept soundly until the next morning.

When he awoke, his own
clothes were nowhere to be seen
but a new, embroidered suit lay
on the chair, in their place. He
dressed himself in the new clothes
and then he set off for the stables,
to see to his horse.

On the way to the stables, the
merchant passed a beautiful
rose garden. The sight of a
white rose bush reminded him
of Beauty's wish and he left
the path to gather a bunch
of the roses.

He had only picked one rose
when he heard a terrible sound
behind him. Turning round
he saw a big beast.

The big beast said, in a big voice, "You ungrateful man! Whose bed did you sleep in? Whose food have you eaten? And whose clothes are you wearing? Mine, mine, mine! And you repay my kindness by stealing my roses. You shall die!"

The big beast looked so fierce that the poor man was terrified.

"Please do not kill me," he begged.

"Your life will be spared on one condition," replied the beast. "You must come back here in a month's time, bringing with you whatever shall first meet you on your return home."

Beauty's father could not do other than agree to this.

As the merchant rode away from the palace, he thought about the promise he had given to the beast.

Then he remembered how Beauty had stood waving to him as he left home. An awful thought struck him. "What if it is Beauty who first greets me on my return?"

Meanwhile, Beauty waited at the window of her room, watching for her dear father to return. When she saw a figure on horseback appear in the distance, she skipped down the garden path.

Yes, it was her dear father returning home, but Beauty could not think what was wrong with him. He looked so tired and sad.

"Father, are you not glad to see me?" asked Beauty.

"Glad? Oh, my little Beauty," cried the poor merchant.

When they reached the cottage, the merchant told his daughter of his promise to the beast. "But you shall not return with me, Beauty, whatever happens," he said.

Beauty, however, insisted that once a promise was made, it should be kept. Finally her father agreed that, at the end of the month, he would take her to the beast.

The end of the month came all too quickly and the merchant and his beloved daughter set off through the woods.

Towards nightfall, Beauty and her father arrived at the palace in the wood. They walked in and found a dainty supper for two was laid out on the table.

As they sat at the table, a terrible sound was heard at the door. It was the beast.

The beast turned to Beauty's father and asked, "Is this the daughter for whom you gathered the white roses?"

"Yes," said the merchant.

"She need not be sorry," said the beast, "for everything in the palace is for her use. Her room is ready now. Goodnight."

When Beauty reached her room, she found it more beautiful than any she had ever seen. Quite tired out, she was soon fast asleep.

In the morning, Beauty and her father had breakfast together. Then they said goodbye. When her father had ridden out of sight, Beauty went to her room. On one wall hung a mirror and beneath it, in letters of gold, was written:

"Little Beauty, dry your eyes,
Needless are those tears and sighs;
Gazing in this looking-glass,
What you wish shall come to pass."

These lines comforted Beauty, for she thought that if she were very unhappy she could wish herself at home again.

The days which followed seemed long to Beauty. Yet the beast had left many things for her amusement.

Sometimes she read and sometimes she painted. Some days she played outside in the gardens and on other days she gathered the beautiful flowers.

Each evening, at supper-time, the same sound was heard at the door and a big voice asked, "May I come in?" And each evening Beauty, trembling, answered, "Yes, Beast." Then they talked together.

Although the beast's body and voice terrified Beauty, his words were so kind that she soon grew less afraid of him.

"Am I very ugly, Beauty?" the beast asked one evening.

"Yes, Beast."

"And very stupid?"

"No, not stupid, Beast."

"Could you love me, Beauty?"

"Yes, I do love you, Beast, for you are so kind."

"Then will you marry me, Beauty?"

"Oh! No, no, Beast."

The beast seemed so unhappy that Beauty felt very miserable. "But I could not marry a beast," she said to herself.

The next morning Beauty looked into her mirror. "I wish I could know how my dear father is," she said. Then, as she gazed into the looking-glass, she saw a sad picture. Her father lay ill in bed and no one was looking after him. Beauty cried all day to think of his pain and his loneliness.

When the beast paid his usual visit in the evening, he saw how sad Beauty looked.

"What is the matter, Beauty?" he asked. She then told him why she was so unhappy and she begged him to let her go home.

"It will break my heart if you go, Beauty," said the beast.

"Yet I cannot bear to see you weep," went on the beast. "You shall go home tomorrow."

"Thank you, Beast," said Beauty, "but I will not break your heart. I shall come back within a week."

The beast looked very doubtful, for he was afraid he was going to lose Beauty for ever.

"Take this ring," he said sadly, "and if you should wish to come back, lay it on your table before you go to bed at night. And now, goodbye, my Beauty."

That night Beauty looked in the mirror and wished that next morning she might wake up in her father's cottage.

Beauty's wish came true, for next morning she found herself at home again.

From the very moment he saw her, Beauty's father began to get better. She could hardly believe it when she found a week had passed. But, although her father was much improved, Beauty did not feel that he was yet well enough to be left with her unkind sisters.

"I shall stay for one more week," said Beauty, and her father smiled happily at this news.

However, only a day or two had passed when Beauty had a dream. She dreamt that the beast was lying on the grass, near the white rose bush in the palace garden. He was saying "Oh! Beauty, Beauty, you said you would come back. I shall die without you."

This dream wakened Beauty and she could not bear to think of the poor beast. She jumped out of bed and laid the magic ring on her table. Then she fell asleep again.

When she woke in the morning, she was in her own room in the beast's palace.

Beauty knew that the beast never came to see her until the evening and yet the day seemed as if it would never end. At last supper-time came, but the beast did not arrive.

Poor Beauty felt miserable. At last a sudden thought struck her. What if her dream was true? What if the beast was lying on the grass near the rose bush?

Beauty ran out into the darkness of the palace garden and made her way towards the white rose bush. There, lying on the wet grass beneath the rose bush, she found the beast. She knelt down beside him on the grass and put her hand on his head. At her touch the beast opened his eyes.

"I cannot live without you, Beauty," he whispered, "so I am starving myself to death. Now that I have seen your face again, I shall die content."

"Oh, dear Beast, I cannot bear it if you die," said Beauty. "Please live and I will marry you. I love you, I really do. You have such a kind heart."

When Beauty had spoken these words, she hid her face in her hands and cried and cried. When she looked up, the beast was gone and a handsome prince stood by her side. He thanked her for freeing him.

"What do you mean?" asked Beauty, surprised. "Oh! I want my Beast, my dear Beast and nobody else!"

Then the prince explained. "A wicked fairy enchanted me and said I must be a beast and seem stupid and ugly," he told her. "Only a beautiful lady who was willing to marry me could break the spell. You are the beautiful lady, Beauty," went on the prince. Then the prince kissed Beauty and led her towards the palace. Soon a good fairy appeared, bringing with her Beauty's father.

Beauty married the prince and, with her dear father near her, lived happily ever after.

A History of Beauty and the Beast

The most well-known version of *Beauty and the Beast* was written by Madame Leprince de Beaumont in 1757. The tale was published in her *Magasin des enfants* and has since gone on to inspire books and films, including Walt Disney's much-loved 1991 animated film.

Leprince de Beaumont's plot features many of the same elements we expect to find in the tale today. There is a merchant with a beautiful daughter, a beast living a solitary life in a large palace and two jealous, self-centred sisters. The tale portrays a kind, beautiful young woman who accepts and loves another, regardless of the beast's appearance.

It further warns readers, through the characters of Beauty's sisters, against personal vanity and sisterly jealousy.

Ladybird's 1967 retelling, written by Vera Southgate is a classic of its time and has helped to bring the story to a new generation.

Collect more fantastic

LADYBIRD 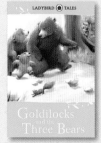 TALES

Little Red Riding Hood
9781409311126

Goldilocks and the Three Bears
9781409311119

Cinderella
9781409311072

Jack and the Beanstalk
9781409311102

The Gingerbread Man
9781409311096

The Three Little Pigs
9781409311089

The Three Billy Goats Gruff
9781409311065

Hansel and Gretel
9781409311133

Puss in Boots
9781409311225

Rapunzel
9781409311195

Rumpelstiltskin
9781409311164

The Elves and the Shoemaker
9781409311188

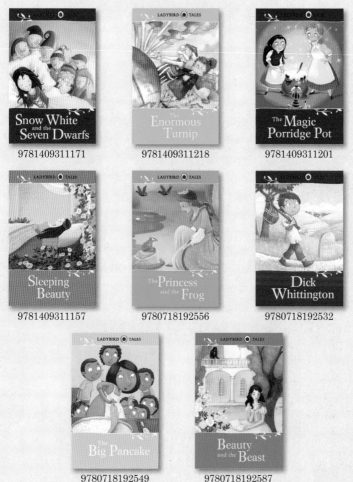

Snow White and the Seven Dwarfs
9781409311171

The Enormous Turnip
9781409311218

The Magic Porridge Pot
9781409311201

Sleeping Beauty
9781409311157

The Princess and the Frog
9780718192556

Dick Whittington
9780718192532

The Big Pancake
9780718192549

Beauty and the Beast
9780718192587

Endpapers taken from series 606d,
first published in 1964

A catalogue record for this book is available from the British Library

Published by Ladybird Books Ltd
80 Strand London WC2R 0RL
A Penguin Company

001

ISBN: 978-0-71819-258-7

Printed in China